# GREATER PORTLAND

# METROPOLITAN PORTRAITS

Metropolitan Portraits explores the contemporary metropolis in its

diverse blend of past and present. Each volume describes a North

American urban region in terms of historic experience, spatial con-

figuration, culture, and contemporary issues. Books in the series

are intended to promote discussion and understanding of metro-

politan North America at the start of the twenty-first century.

*JUDITH A. MARTIN, SERIES EDITOR*

# GREATER

# PORTLAND

Urban Life and Landscape in the Pacific Northwest

CARL ABBOTT

University of Pennsylvania Press | Philadelphia

Copyright © 2001 University of Pennsylvania Press
Printed in the United States of America on acid-free paper


10 9 8 7 6 5 4 3 2 1


Published by
University of Pennsylvania Press
Philadelphia, Pennsylvania 19104–4011


Library of Congress Cataloging-in-Publication Data

Abbott, Carl
  Greater Portland : urban life and landscape in the Pacific Northwest / Carl Abbott.
    p.   cm.
  ISBN 0-8122-3612-2 (cloth);  ISBN 0-8122-1779-9 (pbk.) — (Metropolitan Portraits)
  Includes bibliographical references and index.
    1. City planning—Oregon—Portland Region.   2. Human geography—Oregon—
  Portland Region.   3. City and town life—Oregon—Portland Region.   4. Urban
  landscape architecture—Oregon—Portland Region.   5. Portland Region (Or.)—
  Civilization.   6. Portland Region (Or.)—Social conditions.   I. Title.
  F884.P85 A23   2001
  307.1'416'0979549—dc21                                                  2001-018113

# CONTENTS

# FOREWORD
## JUDITH A. MARTIN

The Metropolitan Portraits Series seeks to understand and describe contemporary metropolitan regions in a fresh manner—one that is informed and informative. Carl Abbott was among the first to answer the call to become part of the Metropolitan Portraits series, and I am grateful for his belief in this effort. This book shares a common thematic structure that will suffuse the series: the inherited land and its contemporary reworking, the effects of important external events, and the power and importance of local cultures. As more volumes emerge, it is hoped that comparisons of many city regions will be possible, despite variations in data and in manner of presentation. *Greater Portland* stands as the latest in Abbott's authoritative work on Portland, this time including the whimsical view through children's literature and through artistic representation.

Abbott shows a Portland being continually refashioned by interactions with present events. He describes the city-region as a destination of promise for people from the Plains and Mountain states, creating a still primarily native-born white residential base. This is a region where geography matters. Nestled within the confines of the Cascades and the Coast Range and shaped by its location at the base of the vast New Deal projects from Bonneville to Grand Coulee, Portland connects outward through the Columbia and Willamette Rivers. The region's early urban specialty of resource processing and export, based on the moist and mild climate for lumbering and farming, continues, while the new economy of electronics, services, and marketing layers on top. Surprisingly, the city region's edges of forest, river, and ocean are publicly controlled. Moreover, the steep hills and narrow valley of the city kept 1960s freeway building close to the old downtown, creating a dense and compact core for a western city.

Abbott organizes the book's cultural analysis within the tension between environmentalism and urbanism, focusing on municipal government as the mediating institution. Portland's famed Urban Growth Boundary is the outside reference, but there is as well the vibrant mix of neighborhood consultation and metropolitan organization.

Abbott then gives us the Portland region as four distinct cultural environments. The first is the neighborhoods of progressive Portland, a base of civic activism formed on 1960s and early '70s battles against an Interstate highway and against urban renewal. Residents here share with other Portlanders an enthusiasm for urban life within the recreational world of bicycles, skis, backpacks, and campers. The second is the "silicon suburbs," principally west of downtown, which most resemble the rest of metropolitan North America. Japanese and American chip and software firms located here now provide more than 61,000 jobs. But Portland's comparatively small size means that many suburbanites maintain a downtown orientation, with few competing new sub-centers.

The third environment is the neighborhoods of multiethnic poverty, some south and close to the river, but mainly concentrated in the north and northeast. These areas are more or less equally white and African American with smaller groups of immigrants, Hispanics, and Native Americans. These groups' uncertain economic circumstances suggest an undercurrent of hard living in this progressive city-region. Finally, in the rural fringe settlements within the region's metropolitan boundaries, old ways and old attitudes, plus elements of Portland's early economy, embody an Old West "go-your-own-way" attitude. Abbott characterizes this tension as the Old West versus the New West.

This able analysis ends with a detailed narrative of Portland's 1970s and '80s political activism, which led to the now famous metropolitan growth boundary. Abbott views this planning experiment as a triumph of the "Portland Way": a willingness to keep talking and a belief that the more inclusive the conversational circle the better. He sees this as a fragile circumstance, and refuses to predict the future.

# Introduction
## Portland's Historical Personality

In 1970 the City of Portland completed the Forecourt Fountain to local applause and national acclaim. Located in an urban renewal district near the southern edge of downtown, the fountain was a carefully crafted landscape that covered an entire city block. Although themselves outsiders to the city, designers Lawrence Halprin and Angela Danadjieva created a distinctive place that is emblematic of Portland's approach to city making, for it holds in tension the distinct values of environmentalism and urbanism.

Set between an office building and a parking garage, this oasis and refuge within the city anchors a series of open spaces that break the monotony of a high-rise urban renewal district. The fountain's sloping contours transform a city block into an analogue of a Cascade Mountain stream. Shrubs and trees create tiny cool glades. Water gathers in narrow channels at the top, tumbles across concrete lips and plates, sloshes around artificial boulders, and plunges into a pool. As viewers drift toward the surging waters, the fountain echoes the Olmstedian goal of urban parks that draw their users away from the city.

The same space is also designed for intense urban use. It serves as a plaza for the Civic Auditorium. Especially in its early years, before growing vegetation began to block sight lines, it was a socially

Ira Keller Fountain (C. Bruce Forster). The Ira Keller Fountain (originally the Forecourt Fountain) was an instant hit with Portlanders and drew praise from design critics around the country. At the fountain's dedication in 1970, one hundred hippies staged a spontaneous "wade in," setting the pattern of intensive use. Designer Lawrence Halprin told the author that he saw in the fountain a "new role model for plazas cum fountains as active participatory centers to be actively used and enjoyed and entered into rather than just visually good looking areas."

charged public space. Businessmen walked out of their way to see the water turned on at 11:00 A.M. Families brought picnics on summer weekends. Hippies bathed in the pools, smoked pot, and drove the city parks commissioner to distraction. The fountain has accommodated rock concerts, ballet performances, baptisms, and weddings.

Contemporary Portland offers other examples and symbols of this creative cohabitation of country and city. Metropolitan area residents voted to tax themselves for the acquisition of stream cor-

INTRODUCTION

ridors, parks, and other open spaces, while the City of Portland continues to add light rail and streetcar lines with their promise to inten-
sify land use. Both officially and unofficially, the city uses two very
different emblems to epitomize its character as a community. One is
the blue heron, adopted as an official city symbol in 1986. This graceful bird that thrives in the riverside marshes wending through the
metropolis seemed a natural mascot to Mayor Bud Clark, who enjoyed early morning canoe trips along the Willamette River. Herons
now appear on city letterhead and microbrewery labels. The other
emblem is a huge hammered copper statue of "Portlandia" reaching
down from a postmodern city office building toward the downtown
bus mall. The figure represents civic life and commerce. Its instal-
lation occasioned a spontaneous community celebration as thousands of Portlanders turned out on a Sunday morning to watch the
statue barged upriver like a red-orange Cleopatra and hoisted onto
its pedestal in the heart of downtown.

This careful balance between environmentalism and urbanism
introduces one of the several creative tensions that have shaped
the character of Portland over the past generation. During the last
quarter of the twentieth century, Portlanders tried to redefine and
bridge a fundamental divide in urban and regional planning. Builders of modern cities have long been torn between the preferences
for "going out" and "going up" — for lowering the overall density of
metropolitan settlements or for increasing the intensity of land use.
In terms of professional planning practice, we see the dichotomy
in the differences between regionwide prescriptive "mapping" of
urban form and detailed small area planning for downtowns and
neighborhoods. In the Portland case, environmentalism as an urban
planning goal draws explicitly on the thought of Frederick Law Olmsted and Lewis Mumford, with their visions of cities and towns interlacing with the natural and cultivated environments in a democratic
regionalism. Portland's eclectic urbanists borrow the insights of
Jane Jacobs and William S. Whyte to assert the value of civic inter-

action in public spaces and the theory of John Stuart Mill to argue the creative and liberating effects of social and cultural diversity.

One result is strong public involvement in both grassroots environmentalism and neighborhood conservation. Small waterways, wetlands, and natural spaces in the Portland area benefit from more than seventy-five "Friends of . . ." organizations. Friends of Forest Park, Friends of Fanno Creek, Friends of the Columbia Slough, Friends of Elk Rock Island, and similar organizations monitor development pressures and advocate for restoration programs. At the same time, Portland hosts two dozen community development corporations and has a national reputation for its network of more than one hundred city-sponsored but community-controlled neighborhood associations.

Such conceptual and practical choices are common to every American metropolis. They are central terms in our planning and policy vocabulary. Yet Portland may be one of the few cities that have actively reconciled their inherent tension. It is one of the few large cities in the United States "where it works," to quote *The Economist* from 1990.[1] It has a long record of appearances near the top of urban livability rankings. An informal poll of planning and design experts by the University of Buffalo in 1988 rated Portland's efforts to deal with urban design issues among the best in the United States, and it continued to impress the progressive architects and planners of the Congress for the New Urbanism when it hosted their year 2000 meeting.[2] The city makes regular appearances as well on lists of the nation's best managed cities.[3]

Indeed, a series of books in the past decade hold up Portland as one American city that is worthy of imitation. Alexander Garvin in *The American City: What Works and What Doesn't* (1996) and Richard Moe and Carter Wilkie in *Changing Places: Rebuilding Community in the Age of Sprawl* (1997) add further praise for its downtown. Robert Kaplan, in *An Empire Wilderness: Travels into America's Future* (1998), notes Portland's choice to swim against the tide of American

INTRODUCTION

development. David Rusk in *Inside Game/Outside Game* (1999) comments that "the best evidence for the success of Portland's growth management policies is the quality of life in so much of the region. It is found in . . . parkland and other natural areas . . . in strong, healthy city neighborhoods. . . . There is a depth and solidity to downtown Portland that compels confidence in its future."

*Utne Reader* in 1997 named Portland the nation's second most "enlightened" town for its "sprawlbusting." Even the curmudgeonly James Howard Kunstler wrote in *The Geography of Nowhere* (1993) that Portland "seems to defy the forces that elsewhere drag American urban life into squalor and chaos. . . . Intelligent planning, plus a little geographical luck" have created a city whose residents "deserve to feel proud."[4]

Taken together, these positive assessments suggest that metropolitan Portland comes close to matching an emerging model of good urban form. Dominating discussion of metropolitan planning and policy in the 1990s, this model embraces a series of normative prescriptions about the characteristics of a balanced metropolis. In particular, it assigns high value to the maintenance of strong downtowns in order to nurture cultural vibrancy, promote social cohesion, and support nationally competitive advanced service industries. Since the landmark 1974 report on *The Costs of Sprawl*, prepared by the Real Estate Research Corporation for the U.S. Environmental Protection Agency, advocates of managed growth have had practical justifications for their argument that the centered metropolis should also be a compact metropolis. Concentrating urbanized land within radial corridors and nodes presumably reduces energy consumption and keeps the infrastructure of roads and utility systems affordable.

Portland as both city and metropolitan region has earned a reputation as a capital of "good planning" for pioneering the actual implementation of this compact city model. In terms of cityscape and urban form, Portland has managed with some success to bring environmentalism and urbanism together in a coherent package of mutually supportive planning and development decisions. The result, in its simplest formulation, is a metropolis that is stronger at its center than at its edges, whether we measure that strength in political clout or the allocation of investment. In political perspective, metropolitan Portland is noteworthy for a political culture that treats land use planning, with its restrictions on private actions, as a legitimate expression of the community interest.

Outside observers have a common agenda. They are trying to determine how Portland might serve as a model or warning for other communities. Political journalist David Broder wrote in 1998 that "Portland has been a pioneer" whose efforts have "implications for communities across the country struggling with problems of traffic and growth, of blighted center city neighborhoods and suburbs encroaching on farms and forests." [5] Vice President Al Gore in 1998 held up Portland as the best of all possible worlds, where quality-of-life planning has stimulated rather than muffled economic growth. George Will soon accused Gore and likeminded folks of gullible "Portland envy," claiming that the city is actually strangling in traffic and drowning in housing price inflation. Free marketeers from the Heritage Foundation and Cato Institute echo Will's complaints, while the *National Review* calls Portland "the Potemkin Village of the smart-growth movement." But Bruce Katz of the Brookings Institution's Center for Urban and Metropolitan Policy writes that Portland is "way ahead of most other places in the country," and architecture professor Roger Lewis says that it is "America's most successful management and urban design model . . . the product of enlightened judgment applied over many decades to wisely accommodate growth within a beautiful landscape." [6]

This search for lessons raises an important question of history and policy: how has a midsized provincial city become a pattern and example? For its first century and quarter (1845–1970), Portland was typical of U.S. cities rather than extraordinary. "You will hear Portland spoken of in some communities on the coast as if it were as old as Rome . . . [with] the ease and comfort of a matured civilization," wrote Walter Hines Page in 1905. The city was described most often as an oasis of refinement in the wild West, as a rather tepid community that avoided extremes that might affect its "conservatism and comfort" (to quote Ray Stannard Baker in 1903).[7] It passed its early decades with less labor-management warfare, ethnic violence, or ostentatious capitalism than San Francisco, Seattle, or Denver. Followers rather than leaders, Portlanders in the early twentieth century imitated eastern models in staging a world's fair, creating a park system, and introducing city planning.

Yet relatively slow growth offered significant advantages to a generation of community leaders who came of age in the 1960s and 1970s. On the one hand, economic stability after the boom of World War II prevented widespread land clearance and fended off the wholesale modernist program of rebuilding the entire city center. On the other hand, stability offered freedom for experimentation to a confident generation nurtured in the national prosperity of 1945–74. Modest size meant that residents could think of the metropolitan area as a single place in need of common solutions; in planning jargon, it was, and still is, "imageable." Racial homogeneity allowed most of these same residents to see themselves as members of a single social community. Portland's curious and antiquated system of nonpartisan commission government offered multiple opportunities for new candidates to introduce new ideas into local politics.

As I write at the beginning of the twenty-first century, the successes of the last generation may be pushing Portland back toward the national norm. Certainly the city has lost some of the funkiness of the 1970s. Rising property values have pushed hippie craftspeople to the outskirts. The bicentennial house on Southeast 20th Avenue that used to greet me with a stars-and-stripes paint job has been rehabbed and repainted a serious monotone by a community development corporation. Traveling blockbuster exhibits at the Portland Art Museum now get more admiration; the historic vacuum cleaner collection and the 24-Hour Church of Elvis receive less. "Good coffee, no backtalk," the twenty-year-old slogan of a local coffee company, may be out of place in a city with sixty Starbucks outlets.

To move from culture to politics, rapid growth has stirred fears that Portland is losing its special livability. "No growth" advocates find a sympathetic hearing when infill development puts row houses on vacant lots, replaces cheap residential hotels with new office towers, and requires the regional government to push the Urban Growth Boundary into berry fields and vegetable farms. Successful planning also attracts ideological challenges from free market advocates, who have had a noticeable impact on land use and transportation policy. The rise of technoentrepreneurship in electronics and software has created wealth that is indifferent to most local political concerns. Many middle class Portlanders remain wedded to low tax/small government populism, a position that draws on a remembered and mythologized heritage of pioneer individualism. But newcomers often bring new talents and a strong desire to preserve the very traits that they found attractive.

I offer this introduction to Portland as a national model that juggles the claims of city and country as a starting point for the book that follows, which tries to assess the "personality" of Portland as it has evolved since the mid-twentieth century. My goal is to write about the relationships between *place* and *people* and the expression of these relationships in *politics* and *policy*. I want to probe interactions between the particularities of Portland's distinctive environment and Portlanders' sense of membership in a metropolitan community. I also use the insights of artists and writers to understand the meanings of place—the ways Portlanders have thought and felt about their metropolitan region. I write about landscape as well as planning regulations, about social changes, community values, and regional culture as well as formal decisions.

Behind these concrete topics will be a concern with two knotty questions. The first: What holds Portlanders together? What are the shared values, common experiences, and distinctive institutions from which Portlanders construct a sense of community? The second: What traits, behaviors and values make metropolitan Portland's six counties—Multnomah, Washington, Clackamas, Clark, Columbia, Yamhill—different from other places? What sets Portlanders apart from the people of similar regional centers such as Indianapolis or Kansas City?

We can address these questions because we already understand the basic outline of Portland's development. Standard urban historical portraits—often called urban biographies—take the process of city building as their narrative line. They focus on the interaction of economic activity, in-migration, physical development, civic organization, and government. They take the economic/physical city as the framework within which we understand the growth of public and private institutions, neighborhoods, ethnic groups, and social classes. This is a grand theme. It is important to know, for example, how and why Seattle came to be the great city of Puget Sound, or how New York pushed past Philadelphia as the national metropolis and coped with the problems of growth. This is the narrative line that organizes local history museum exhibits, including the "Portland!" exhibit at the Oregon Historical Society. It organizes three essential books on Portland power, politics, and growth by E. Kimbark Mac-Coll and Harry Stein and the Pulitzer prize winning history of Gotham by Ed Burrows and Mike Wallace.[8]

Urban biography is an essential first step, but contemporary urbanized regions, which may stretch 50 miles across (Portland), 100 miles across (Philadelphia), or even 150 miles across (Los Angeles) are unified and divided on new principles. The most important divisions among metropolitan residents may now arise from religion (liberal and traditional worldviews), from suburb-to-suburb competition, or from industrial affiliation (Los Angeles garment workers versus Los Angeles entertainment entrepreneurs). Indeed, each of us knows and uses certain parts of the metropolitan area and ignores others, living in regions of our own devising. The ways these personalized spatial worlds relate to each other are creating larger metropolitan patterns that we are still struggling to understand. In effect, our project is to make more visible the invisible patterns of daily life.

For Portland, the central challenge is to understand the ways that landscape and history have interacted to shape a particular urban community into a metropolitan area with some significantly "un-American" characteristics. The "politics of growth" will never be far from my mind. The political processes of coalition building, civic leadership, and elections can find expression in something as specific as planning responses to listings of fish runs under the Endangered Species Act. But politics can also be as broad as the changing social patterns and cultural preferences that have shaped the economy and cityscape to meet changing understandings of the good city over the generations.

In thinking about the history and character of Portland at the turn of a new century, I have identified several characteristics and tensions that serve as windows into the Portland experience. These are some of the themes, issues, or contradictions that have made the city-region of Portland what it is.

Portland offers a paradoxical balancing of past and future. Unlike Las Vegas or San Jose, it is not a place that is always on fast forward. One reason the city is so widely admired today is that it looks and works much like a city of the 1950s. One of its radical virtues, in other words, has been to conserve or even recreate the best from previous generations of city making while accommodating economic and demographic change. In part this is the result of happy accident. Portland has generally avoided a boom/bust economy. Instead, decades of growth have been followed by decades of consolidation. In the Pacific Northwest, Seattle has been the hare

The Portland Building (Oregon Historical Society Neg. 80983). Built in the early 1980s after a national design competition, architect Michael Graves's Portland Building put the city on the map of the postmodern aesthetic. Its eastern facade towers above Lownsdale and Chapman squares, the city's major gathering places of the nineteenth century, and dwarfs the bronze elk given to the city by an enthusiastic mayor in 1900—a reminder that the animals once descended from the West Hills to browse the flats along the Willamette. "Portlandia" occupies a second-floor niche on the building's west facade.

and Portland the tortoise. Stewart Holbrook put it this way 1952, in *Far Corner: A Personal View of the Pacific Northwest*: "The character of Seattle is simple and crystal-clear. Seattle is a place of singleness of mind. The idea is always a Bigger and Better Seattle." In contrast, "Portland presents a civic character of complexities . . . though many of its leading men have wanted the place to become another New York or Chicago, just as many others have been quite content with the status of the moment, whether that moment was 1850, 1900, or 1950."[9]

Nevertheless, the Portland region of 2001 is also a very different place from the city of the Eisenhower years. After a generation of rapid social and economic change, Portland displays the tensions between old and new economies. The business section of the *Ore-*

*gonian* is full of news about Silicon Forest investment, software startups, and airline routes to Asia. The sports section is heavy on hunting and fishing information. The city grew on the "Old West" economy of resource production and direct resource processing; its manufacturing base was wood products and furniture, flour, meat, and woolen goods. To the old economy has been added an overlay of the new information economy, with electronics and professional services. Portland's high-rise downtown thus lies next to industrial sanctuary districts full of warehouses and light manufacturing. It sees itself as the capital of the wild—that is, natural—West. But it also envisions a future as a generator of intellectual products and services. This tension is not new. More than fifty years ago, Richard Neuberger described Portland to readers of the *Saturday Evening Post* in 1947 as a town with a "split personality. It can't quite make up its mind whether to be a swashbuckling industrial giant . . . or a landed squire pruning rosebushes and meditatively watching salmon ascend to their mountain spawning grounds. . . . Portland is a mixture of the rustic and the metropolitan." [10]

Closely related to the economic contrast is the challenge of balancing the values of city and country—the challenge that opened this introduction. Portlanders have managed to create an urbane metropolis at the same time that many residents see easy access to the natural environment as its greatest asset. Portland is known both for its thriving and lively downtown and older neighborhoods and for its least settled sections of protected farmland, wetlands, and 3000-acre Forest Park. The city is carefully "placed" within its landscape, and residents of the region wrestle with reconciling complex and contradictory claims to the use of its rivers, valleys, mountains, and biotic communities. It is a "provincial city" in the literal sense of finding its regional connections to be sources of identity, self-satisfaction, and occasional embarrassment.

There is also embarrassment lurking in the city's history. Any realistic assessment of the contemporary metropolis must weigh

Portland's progressive reputation against its strong, historically rooted social conservatism. For one example, Portland has been a white person's city for most of its history (from early territorial laws against African Americans to the KKK in the 1920s, anti-Japanese sentiment in the 1940s, and skinhead violence in the 1980s). It has been conservative in social styles and stingy in the arts and philanthropy. Oregon in 1996 ranked twenty-fifth among the states in adjusted gross income but fortieth in itemized charitable contributions per income tax return, although charitable giving has been on the rise.[11]

Portland's civic and commercial leaders have sometimes been smugly satisfied with their community. Portland may have lost out to Seattle in the contest for economic primacy in the Northwest, but its next serious regional challenger is Salt Lake City, eight hundred miles away across multiple mountain ranges and sagebrush plains. Historian Kimbark MacColl has noted its tendency to "solidness, venerability, dignity, conservatism."[12] Conservative values have meant moderation in politics, a commitment to conserving the natural surroundings, high levels of satisfaction with the status quo, and a persistent reluctance to fund public services and facilities (although parks measures do well). A journalist wrote in the 1930s, "To know what Portland would do under the stress of any given circumstance, it is only necessary to imagine how Calvin Coolidge would act."[13]

One further tension in Portland results from the effort to balance two visions of the regional and national future. Portlanders have always felt blessed by the wealth of nature; they assume and expect unimpeded access to the outdoors for both resource production and recreation. But the regional landscape also generates a sense of limits; tall mountains and thick clouds are symbolic reminders that the natural world is a finite system that places limits on human aspiration. The ever present call of the wild (or at least the call of the woods) pulls Portlanders toward enjoyment at the expense of ambition. We don't work so hard that we are not able to enjoy the city and region, starting work at 8:00 A.M. but knocking off early on Fridays and summer evenings. "Slowness," a trait noted a century ago, wars with the fast-track computer and Internet economy that is also well represented in Portland. Venture capitalists sometimes decide that Portland entrepreneurs, especially in comparison to the denizens of Silicon Valley, are not hungry enough to merit their investment. Residents recognize that population growth provides the market base for high culture and sophisticated consumption—symphony, art galleries, restaurants—but don't want a city that overwhelms its setting.

The book is organized in three broad topical chapters: Place, People, and Plans. The first chapter asks how Portland's setting and landscape have shaped the city's economy and values, culture and expectations. The second explores how personal values, race, and industrial affiliation (logger, lawyer, software writer) have created several distinct communities of interest and how these are located within the metropolitan area. The third asks how Portlanders are consciously shaping their place through planning and policy, in effect reversing the approach of Chapter 1.

Each of these broad topics—natural environment and economy, social and cultural ecology, civic environment—is framed in the context of regional history. They are explored at the micro scale of districts and neighborhoods, at the middle scale of the city and its six-county metropolitan area, and at the macro scale of relationships between the metropolitan area and the greater Northwest—hinterland, weekendland, raincoast, Cascadia.

Many people think that Portland is at its best in the small pleasures: downtown squares and streetcar era shopping districts, fountains and parks, coffeehouses and microbreweries, bookstores and bike paths, neighborhoods like St. Johns and Brooklyn that have a modest but firm sense of self. In part because each district has its own character and sense of place, many Portlanders cling to the

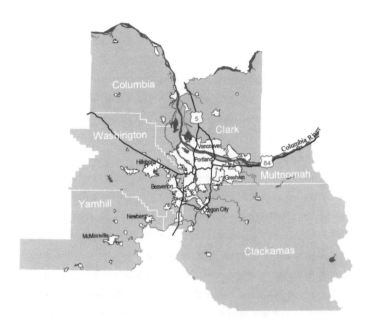

Cities and counties in the Portland area (Irina Sharkova, Portland State University). The Portland area includes the central city, with more than 500,000 residents as of 2000, four cities with populations of 90,000 to 138,000, and fifteen other towns with populations greater than 10,000.

notion that they live in an overgrown town and not, heaven forbid, a "big city." "Portland remains casual, friendly, and above all, available," writes slacker generation *Monk* magazine. "Seattle has gotten a bit more distant, fast-paced, and grown-up." [14] But preserving that detailed urban fabric requires thinking, planning, and acting on behalf of a far larger region. Indeed, one of the most telling criticisms of the Portland metropolis has been a frequent failure to dream big dreams.

Portland has nationally admired institutions for citizen involvement and civic action, but the viability of its political culture is continually under challenge from tides of in-migration and the values of privatism. The metro area has certainly felt the national disengagement from public life and withdrawal from traditional community organizations that political scientist Robert Putnam has summarized as the trend toward "bowling alone." Portlanders must continually tend and maintain their forums and institutions for civic discourse and community action and educate their neighbors about the processes of civic involvement. The city's traditional frugality and its caution about change have often led to inaction and missed opportunities

Portland's contradictory sense of self is expressed in the ways residents represent their metropolis to themselves and the world. A neighborhood statue of Paul Bunyan looks to the past, while copperclad "Portlandia" looks to a more sophisticated future. Pictures of the growing downtown skyline contrast with postcard views of Mount Hood looming over the city. The families of Beverly Cleary's children's books about Henry Huggins and Ramona Quimby are far different from the colorful workingmen of Stewart Holbrook's regional history, the social misfits of Gus Van Sant's 1989 movie *Drugstore Cowboy*, or the old Wobblies in Gary Snyder's poetry. In Portland, in short, we see multiple meanings of community, multiple understandings of the future, and multiple uses of the past in service to that future.

# Capital of the Columbia

## A HARD GREEN LAND

Mount Hood hovers over Portland like a watchful god.

The iconic view of many cities features a skyline or a manmade feature — an Eiffel Tower, Gateway Arch or Brandenburger Tor, Transamerica Tower or Empire State Building.

In place of cathedral spire or capitol dome, Portland offers its natural setting. "The mountain is out," we say when the winter clouds clear and Mount Hood shimmers white in the afternoon sun. Snowmelt from the mountain's northwestern valleys flows pure and untreated through Portland water taps. We worry occasionally, when small tremors shake the still living volcano, that Hood may suddenly erupt as Mount St. Helens did in 1980; geologists have mapped the most likely course of lava and ash flows toward Portland's eastern suburbs. But usually the mountain is playground and backdrop, silhouetted against a sharp blue dawn on occasional clear winter mornings, tinged pink in summer evening sunsets. "The white mountain loomed like Truth itself, or a bad painting," was novelist Robin Cody's capsule summary in *Ricochet River*.[1]

Portland's other icon is roses. Some places may identify with the hard and heavy products of industry as Iron City or Motown. Portland identifies with tens of thousands of rose bushes in city parks

Mount Hood from Washington Park (Livable Oregon, Inc.). Portlanders mark the weather and the seasons by the face of Mount Hood on the eastern horizon—floating over a sea of low clouds or glistening with new snow, backed by the colors of a winter sunrise or bathed in the softer glow of a summer evening.

and front yards. As early as 1889, lawyer and litterateur C. E. S. Wood suggested an annual rose show. Civic leaders and journalists made Portland the "Rose City" by the new century and were soon promoting an annual Rose Festival, complete with parades, queen, and Royal Rosarians to oversee the festivities. Long after cities such as Denver and Los Angeles have given up their turn of the century promotional festivals, Portland still stages the Rose Festival each June. Bright red roses are painted on the doors of city vehicles, bracketing the slogan "The City That Works." Even police cars sport their own red rose decals.

The common photo for tourist brochures and business promotion booklets combines the two images. Photographers set their tripods in the Washington Park rose gardens just west of the central business district. Roses grace the foreground while downtown buildings frame and support the image of the mountain, made to float over the city through the power of the telephoto lens. Although its peak is fifty miles from downtown Portland, the mountain rises more than 11,000 feet above the city—a greater upward reach than Long's Peak above Estes Park, Colorado, and only a few hundred feet short of the rise of the Jungfrau over Interlaken. Mike Burton, executive director of Metro, Portland regional government, claims that Portland's vision for the future can be summed in two phrases: "everyone can see Mount Hood" balanced by "every child can walk to a library." [2]

The rose cult(ivation) is a function of the marine climate of western Oregon. Portland lies within the northwestern rain coast that stretches from Mendocino, California to the Alaskan islands, an area whose extremes of weather are defined by wet and dry far more than by cold and hot. Its cousins are other locations on western coasts and in the middle latitudes, where prevailing westerly winds squeeze moisture from maritime polar air masses but where proximity to the oceans moderates the range of temperatures. Portlanders would feel at home in southern Chile, Tasmania, Norway, northern Spain, France, and the British Isles. Its peers are Seattle

"Wind from the South" (Stephen Leflar, etching, 1984, Visual Chronicle of Portland). Rain in Portland arrives from the southeast with counterclockwise winds from low pressure centers over the Pacific. In the showery season from February to June, bands of rain alternate with clear skies, a weather pattern Stephen Leflar captures in this view southward toward downtown and the west hills.

and Victoria, Wellington and Hobart, Bilbao, Bordeaux, and Bristol. The cult of roses reflects not only the cultural Anglophilia of late nineteenth-century Americans but also a commonality of ecosystems. It is not pure puffery for the wine industry that has developed in Portland's southwestern exurbs since the 1970s to note that northern Oregon and southern France have the same latitude.

Portlanders watch the northern Pacific for their weather. The season of storms arrives in late October or November when low pressure builds in the Gulf of Alaska and the jet stream drops southward to sweep across the northern states. The counterclockwise swirl around the deep atmospheric low pumps moist Pacific air across Oregon from the west and southwest, driving ashore band after band of clouds. "Pineapple express" is the shorthand for especially

CHAPTER 1

juicy storms of warmer air that pick up moisture from as far to the southwest as Hawai'i and drench the valleys and mountains.

Heavy storms abate in February, giving way to a long showery season from February through June. Spring comes early, with crocuses in February and daffodils in bloom by early or mid-March, followed by fruit trees, azaleas, rhododendrons, and then roses in time for the June celebration. Sunny days alternate with days of clouds and rain, sunny hours with showers, balmy weeks with chilly weeks as late as May. Spring flowers last for weeks in the cool and damp.

The sun comes out and stays in July, August, September, and into October. A ridge of high pressure builds northward from California, displacing the winter low and pushing the jet stream over Canada. The prevailing clockwise winds are now from the northwest, bringing cool but relatively dry marine air to chill the Oregon coast and filter up the Columbia River to Portland. Only 6 percent of Portland's precipitation falls in the summer. At 46 degrees north latitude (the same as Frederickton, New Brunswick), Portland is scarcely the land of midnight sun, but summer light lasts appreciably longer than in the American heartland along the Ohio River or Chesapeake Bay.

Cool, dry summers and wet, mild winters combine to give northwestern North America the greatest conifer forests in the world. Deciduous trees in natural stands are confined to lowlands, stream margins, and other moist and sheltered sites. The coastal mountains and Cascades are covered with thick forests of hemlock, cedar, noble fir, and Douglas fir. Waxy needles conserve water in the dry summer; conical crowns take maximum advantage of oblique winter sunlight for continuing photosynthesis. The Northwest's conifers have a 1000 to 1 margin in timber volume over its deciduous trees.

The last weeks of dry summers can also bring fierce forest fires. When high pressure drifts southwest from central Canada and stalls over Idaho, the hot, dry air of the continental interior pours through the Columbia River Gorge, pushing Portland temperatures through the 90s and over 100. Hot haze settles in over the city and householders wish for air conditioning, a rarity in all but the newest houses.

When the heat persists, dry brush in forest understories can feed wind-fanned blazes. Embedded in the community memory of Portland is the Tillamook Burn of August 1933, when friction from a log chain torched 400-year-old forests in the Coast Range west of Portland. The 1933 fire burned for twenty-three days and ravaged 240,000 acres. Repeated fires in 1939, 1945, and 1951 consumed the baked snags and sticks and added new acres for a total burned-over district of 352,000 acres. The state acquired the desolate lands in the 1940s. Historian Robert Ficken remembers "the truly awesome Tillamook Burn" from trips between the Willamette Valley and the coast in the 1950s: "For mile after mile, the Wilson River Highway [Oregon 6] offered bleak backseat views of ash, blackened snags, and ruined trestlework."[3] Between 1950 and 1970, 25,000 school children helped replant the burn and fixed the story of fire, community effort, and regeneration in popular memory. "Plant trees and grow citizens" was the slogan. Oregon poet William Stafford reflected years later on the devastation:

These mountains have heard God;
they burned for weeks. He spoke
in a tongue of flame from sawmill trash
and you can see His word down to the rock.[4]

Fires notwithstanding, the most common understanding of Portland's climate is grayness. Because the sunny weeks of August lack even the drama of lightning storms, it is the low winter sky that attracts notice—the gray blanket of drizzle, the short winter light. Clouds are great gray sponges wrung out against the west slope of the Cascades. The winter weather can nourish deep depression. But the gray months can also be soothing, muffling, twilight weather, thinking weather. Portlanders outpace most of the nation in magazine subscriptions. They are avid bookworms and science fiction fans who spend 37 percent more than average Americans on reading matter. In the nineteenth century Portland jurist Mathew Deady famously described his city as the place whose "good citizens will sleep sounder and live longer than the San Franciscans."[5]

Portland writers freight the rain with larger meanings. David James Duncan offered up the rain as comforter in *The River Why* (1983): "It was the first good rain since the August showers. . . . A rain that hummed on the river pool and pattered on new puddles. . . . I was lulled and cradled, caressed and enveloped in a cool, mothering touch. . . . I realized that I *had* been given a spirit-helper: I had been given this rain."[6] In Shelley's "Ozymandias," drifting sand and time are the great levelers. "I am the grass. Let me work," wrote prairie-born Carl Sandburg to invoke the power of nature over vanity. Rain does the same work in William Stafford:

**"MY PARTY THE RAIN"**

Loves upturned faces, laves everybody,
applauds tennis courts, pavements; its fingers
ache and march through the forest numbering
limbs, animals, Boy Scouts; it recognizes
every face, the blind, the criminal,
beggar or millionaire, despairing child,
minister cloaked; it finds all the dead
by their stones or mounds, or their deeper listening
for the help of such rain, a census that cares
as much as any party, neutral in politics.

It proposes your health, Governor, at the Capitol;
licks every stone, likes the shape of our state.
Let wind in high snow this year
legislate its own mystery: our lower winter

rain feathers in over miles of trees

to explore. A cold, cellophane layer,

silver wet, it believes what it touches,

and goes on, persuading one thing at a time,

fair, clear, honest, kind—

a long session, Governor. Who knows the end? [7]

Northwestern America is storm coast as well as rain coast. Portland's location promises a reliable cycle of violent weather, a *regular* harshness that stems from the hydrologic cycle of the North Pacific. Duncan's soft rains of early October soon give place to pelting coastal gales. Equinoctial gales roar up the Willamette Valley every fall. The Columbus Day storm of 1962, with hurricane force winds, is remembered each anniversary. January ice storms coat the roads and trees when the wet marine air collides with continental cold at the mouth of the Columbia River Gorge, shutting off the lights and closing down highways and runways.

It is no accident that Oregon writers choose storms as the introductions and pivots of their great regional novels. Cold driving rains control the coastwise trek of an old mountain man in Don Berry's *Trask* (1960). A torrential downpour launches the wanderings of young Clay Calvert in H. L. Davis's Pulitzer prize novel *Honey in the Horn* (1935): "Even to a country accustomed to rain, that was a storm worth gawking at." *Sometimes a Great Notion* (1964), Ken Kesey's sprawling novel about independent loggers on the Oregon coast, begins with water: "Along the western slopes of the Oregon Coastal Range . . . come look: the hysterical crashing of tributaries as they merge into the Wakonda Auga River." Hank Stamper battles the surging river year after year to save his family's waterfront house. When everyone else has moved sensibly uphill, he armors the riverbank like a battleship: "The house protrudes out into the river on a peninsula of its own making, on an unsightly jetty of land shored up on all sides with logs, ropes, cables, burlap bags filled with cement and rocks, welded irrigation pipe, old trestle girders, and bent train rails. . . . And all of this haphazard collection is laced together and drawn back firm against the land by webs of rope and log chain."[8] He carries on family tradition by logging the watershed of the Wakonda Auga, as defiant of labor unions and large corporations as he is of the river. At the book's climax, Hank watches helplessly as Joe Ben Stamper lies pinned in the river under a log that jumped the wrong way, waiting for the turning tide to fill his lungs.

Kesey and Davis and Berry remind their readers of the constant dangers of the recreational environment. Portlanders are safe from Texas tornados and Carolina hurricanes, but they die each year trying to enjoy the outdoors. They capsize while rafting and kayaking rivers that flood with unanticipated rains and snowmelt. They drown while swimming in suburban streams that are far less placid than their surfaces. They die on the Pacific beaches, pulled to sea by sneaker waves or crushed under huge snags shifted suddenly by the surf. Ten thousand people scale Mount Hood each year, but climbers perish in avalanches and whiteouts and missteps on rotten snow. They slip on damp trails and mossy rocks and fall to the water-slicked rocks below. They venture to the forest on bright October days to cut firewood and die when wind snaps a snag or swings a chainsawed tree in an unexpected direction.

Western Oregon has always been a land of physical challenge. Oregon Trail pioneers of the 1840s who reached The Dalles in October faced a painful choice before they could gain the promised Eden of the Willamette Valley. They could pick a way around the south side of Mount Hood before snow and mud closed the passes or lash together unwieldy rafts to launch into the rapids of the rain-swollen Columbia. The last hundred miles to the Willamette Valley could take a month of sodden misery.

The environs of Portland in the late nineteenth and early twentieth centuries were a land of rugged loggers, mill hands, railroad crews, bindle stiffs, Scandinavian gillnetters, and Chinese salmon cannery workers (until they were displaced by packing machines known as Iron Chinks). There were Finnish socialists in Astoria, homegrown populists in Portland, and a scattering of Wobblies in the woods. When farmers had their harvests in and no longer needed field hands, when bad weather closed the logging camps and shut down railroad building, seasonal workers drifted into Portland.

Most of the seasonal workers wintered over in a bachelor neighborhood that stretched a mile along the downtown waterfront. They bought new gear, enjoyed clean beds before they drank up their wages, and ended up sleeping in a flophouse or in the back room of one of Portland's two hundred saloons. To find men without families, Portlanders needed only to follow loud music and the smell of stale beer to waterfront blocks between Everett and Jackson streets. From the Lownsdale district on the south to the Burnside district on the north, this skid road was a neighborhood of lodging houses and flophouses, second hand stores, missions, saloons, brothels, and employment agencies. At its height between 1900 and 1925, the district may have housed as many as 10,000 men, giving Portland proportionately one of the largest skid roads in the country.

In the very middle was Chinatown, serving the same sorts of migratory workers but held distinct in the minds of white Portlanders. Swollen by refugees from anti-Chinese violence in Tacoma and Seattle in 1885–86, the city's Chinese population grew from 1700 in 1880 to 7800 by 1900. The ornate wrought iron balconies and paper lanterns of Chinatown gave a touch of mystery to the brick buildings of First and Second Streets. Like the adjacent Lownsdale and Burnside districts, Chinatown was a nearly all male society with a handful of merchants and thousands of workingmen. The lives of its Chinese-born workers involved activities that white society defined as vices, particularly gambling and the use of opium. Police officials could stand foursquare for virtue by raiding fan tan rooms and opium parlors while ignoring the far more numerous gambling joints and saloons with white customers. Chinatown's very exis-

Chinatown (Oregon Historical Society Neg. 3880). Chinese immigrants to Portland congregated along the central downtown waterfront, where they adapted older commercial buildings with balconies and decorations. Once the second largest on the west coast, Portland's Chinatown dwindled with the curtailment of immigration. During and after World War II, Chinese businesses moved north of Burnside Street into buildings left vacant by the wartime relocation of Japanese Americans.

tence gave Portlanders of European heritage the thrill of confronting the "other" while remaining firmly in charge.

This workingmen's neighborhood has long tied the genteel commercial city to the rough culture of unmarried workers. The Portland Ministerial Association in 1893 and the Portland Vice Commission in 1912 both found that Portland's most prominent families were the landlords for gambling dens and after-hours booze joints. Such capitalists had little interest in closing down the rum business or the sex trade. Transformation came instead from the larger economic force of mechanization, which gradually cut the need for unskilled farm and forest workers.

Just when the last store selling work boots and clothing shut down in the 1980s, a new wave of mobile Mexicans and Central

Japanese American Historical Plaza (Robert Murase Associates). The Japanese American Historical Plaza (1990), a realized dream of Portland businessman and civic leader Bill Naito, sits between busy Front Avenue (now officially Naito Parkway) and a heavily used riverside walkway. On warm days the grassy banks that frame the Plaza are occupied by Latino workingmen while upscale professionals jog past after work. Like many other Portland spaces, it is a visually compelling landscape that has been appropriated for everyday use.

Americans gave another life to the area. The district has shrunk from a mile to a few blocks north of Burnside Street, charity shelters have replaced flophouses, and cocaine has replaced opium as an item of commerce between the seamy and sober sides of Portland. Even so, hobos still wait out rainy weeks in rude camps under the shelter of bridge ramps, missions offer a meal and a prayer, and Spanish-speaking workers help fill the city's need for casual laborers.

Let's pause at the northern end of Tom McCall Waterfront Park on a late spring afternoon. Here along Front Avenue and the remnants of skid road are old and new Portland side by side. In the 1970s the riverside park replaced a six-lane expressway, which in turn had replaced outmoded docks and warehouses three decades earlier. Residents from new middle class housing built on the old Northern Pacific rail yards now jog along the esplanade. High school skateboarders and punksters hang out in the shade of the Burnside Bridge. Unemployed men and Latino laborers rest on the grass. Around them are the granite slabs of the Japanese American Historical Plaza, each engraved with short poems by Oregonian Lawson Inada that tell the story of immigration, wartime deportation, and return.

**Mighty Willamette!**
**Beautiful friend,**
**I am learning,**
**I am practicing**
**To say your name.**

**Black smoke rolls**
**Across the blue sky.**
**Winter chills our bones.**
**This is Minidoka.**

**With new hope,**
**We build new lives.**
**Why complain when it rains.**
**This is what it means to be free.**

## WHERE THE RIVERS CROSS

Weather makes Oregon's rivers, and the rivers have made Portland.

The metropolitan region lies at a natural intersection. Running east to west is the valley of the Columbia River. Extending north to south is the Puget-Willamette Trough, where fault lines have dropped great blocks of land below the parallel coastal mountains and Cascades. To the north, the Trough drops below sea level to form Puget Sound and the Strait of Georgia. Further south it has captured rivers that drain the western sides of the Cascades, diverting the Cowlitz River southward in Washington and the Willamette River northward in Oregon. Even the powerful Columbia bends north between its confluence with the Willamette, where it enters the Trough, and the Cowlitz, where it turns again to exit to the sea.

Mountain snowpack and spring rains stoke these rivers. The Willamette drains the western slopes of the Cascades and the eastern side of the Coast Range. The Columbia rises on the western slope of the northern Rockies in British Columbia, Montana, and Idaho. It absorbs the waters of the Okanagan River and the Clark Fork and the Kootenay River, the 1038-mile Snake, the Yakima, the John Day, and the Deschutes before it cuts through the remarkable passage of the Columbia River Gorge to reach Portland and take in the Willamette. Every spring, state officials measure the depth of snow to let city water managers and irrigation districts plan for lean or fat years, skiers decide when to rack their equipment in the basement, and dam operators map out reservoir discharges to maintain electrical generation and fish runs. The Willamette's average flow is 24 million acre feet per year. The Columbia's annual discharge at its mouth is 180 million acre feet—70 percent of the flow of the Great Lakes-St. Lawrence system and 40 percent of the flow of the Mississippi. A good match for the Columbia is the Danube, which draws the same volume of water from a comparably sized drainage basin.

The Cascade Range itself is a line of volcanic peaks connected by saddles of ancient lava flows. In Washington the peaks are Baker, Rainier, St. Helens, and Adams. In Oregon they are Hood, Jefferson, the Three Sisters, and Crater Lake, the shattered remnant of Mount Mazama. Lassen and Shasta complete the line-up in northern California. Just offshore is the Cascadia Subduction Zone, where the eastward moving Juan de Fuca plate slowly grinds beneath the North American continental plate. Far below the surface, the subduction melts rock to feed volcanic eruptions. Caught by friction, the North American plate gradually bulges upward until pressure is released with a jerk that drops the surface in a magnitude 8 or 9 earthquake.

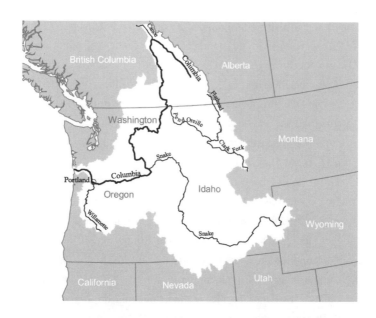

Columbia River system (Irina Sharkova, Portland State University). Dam building from the 1930s to the 1970s made barge traffic possible as far inland as Pasco, Washington on the Columbia River and Lewiston, Idaho on the Snake River. Both the Northern Pacific and Union Pacific Railroads reached—and still reach—western ports through the Columbia River Gorge east of Portland.

The last giant quake was approximately three centuries ago, leaving its traces in drowned coastal forests and marshes.

The Columbia and the Willamette were avenues of exploration, pathways for Anglo-American settlement, and arteries of commerce that made—and still make—Portland the commercial gateway to the American northwest.

The peoples of the North Pacific in the late eighteenth and early nineteenth centuries were swirled by a vortex of imperial ambitions. Up the coast from Mexico and California came Spanish explorer Bruno Heceta (1775). Russian fur traders moved south from Kodiak and Baranof islands. James Cook (1778) and George Vancouver (1791) explored the North American coast for Britain. New England and British traders opened a commerce in furs with China, enlisting crewmen in the islands of Hawai'i (hence the name of the Owyhee River in dry eastern Oregon). American Robert Grey entered the Columbia River in 1792, and British officer William Broughton explored far enough upriver to see and name Mount Hood. Soon thereafter, Canadians and Americans probed transcontinental routes: Alexander Mackenzie in 1793, Meriwether Lewis and William Clark in 1804–6, David Thompson in 1811.

Efforts to establish a permanent presence soon followed. Fur trading companies followed with a short-lived American post at Astoria (1811–13) and a British Hudson's Bay Company post nearby at Fort George. The United States and Britain agreed in 1818 to joint occupation the Oregon Country (the future Oregon, Washington, Idaho, southern British Columbia, and corners of Montana and Wyoming). In 1825, John McLoughlin relocated the regional Hudson's Bay headquarters to a new site at Fort Vancouver, the nucleus for the present city of Vancouver, Washington, across the Columbia River from Portland.

The Hudson's Bay men were claiming ownership of a territory that already served thousands of native villagers. Between Celilo Falls (The Dalles) and the mouth of the Columbia, speakers of Chinook dialects dotted the river islands and entry points of small rivers and streams. Their "metropolis" was Sauvie Island and the adjacent Oregon shore. Lewis and Clark counted 2400 people on the island and 1800 along the south side of the Multnomah Channel. Six years later, British fur trader Robert Stuart reported a population of about 2000 on the island itself—a denser population than the island supports today.[9] By piecing together the reports of different European travelers, we can locate about fifteen separate villages on Sauvie Island and immediately adjacent areas. Residents fished for salmon, sturgeon, and smelt; hunted migratory birds and deer; gathered nuts and berries; and dug wappatoo roots along the rivers. "Wappato Island" was Lewis and Clark's name for Sauvie

Island. Cedar logs provided materials for canoes, cooking utensils, and longhouses. Villages were built to last for years rather than decades, for the abundance of natural resources made it easy for a group to move from one spot to another within its general territory.

In contrast to their bustling settlements along the Columbia, Native Americans made only limited use of the lower Willamette River. Not until they reached the Clackamas River and the Willamette River falls, twenty-five miles upstream, did European explorers find more than scattered and often temporary settlements. Here, where the salmon stopped, the natural environment again made life relatively easy for the Cushook, Chahcowah, and Clackamas peoples. The falls were a point of contact between maritime tribes and the hunting peoples of the Tualatin Valley. Twenty or so small villages of Tualatin Indians used the valley, traded with river people, and occasionally gathered near Gaston. They were a subgroup of the Kalapooias of the central Willamette Valley, all of whom had learned to improve their environment with periodic fires. Their purpose, they told naturalist David Douglas, was to clear the land for ease of gathering wild foods and to force deer into tree islands where they were easy to hunt.

The growing presence of white traders introduced a very different change in the natural environment. Among the world's most isolated peoples, the Indians of the Northwest coast were highly susceptible to the new diseases that arrived with the Europeans. In 1829 measles attacked the Sauvie Island villages. The next year the "Cold Sick" or "Intermitting Fever" appeared in Chinook and Kalapooia villages and raged for the next three years along the Willamette and lower Columbia. It is likely that the disease was malaria brought from the tropical Pacific by traders, although influenza is another possibility. Whatever its true identity, the Cold Sick spread outward from an infection epicenter at Sauvie Island and Fort Vancouver. It killed half in some villages, 90 percent in others, leaving a few hundred Native Americans and a virtually unoccupied landscape for the

English-speaking settlers who began to arrive over the Oregon Trail in the 1840s.

To understand the initial settlement patterns of those pioneers, it is important to remember that explorers and settlers traveled by water whenever possible. The closest contemporary equivalent to the landscape that greeted them in the vicinity of Portland would be the less developed banks of the lower Columbia River. What visitors saw were low, sandy islands, separated by shallow channels from marshy bottomlands and backed by rising hills or bluffs. Most prominent for Portland were Swan Island, Ross Island, and Sauvie Island. Along the riverbanks were thick tangles of willows, cottonwoods, vine maples, ash, and alders. Other wetlands had formed where streams emptied into the Willamette, such as the mouth of Sullivan's Gulch on the east side and Marquam Gulch on the west side. As they approached this marshy, sandy front door, the first Anglo-American settlers found little to praise. Philadelphia physician and naturalist John Townsend summed up a common reaction when he wrote about the future vicinity of Portland that "there is not sufficient extent unencumbered [by vegetation], or which could be fitted for the purposes of tillage, in a space of time short enough to be serviceable; others are at some seasons inundated, which is an insurmountable objection." [10]

To make the scene even less attractive, many of the wider bottomlands were covered with shallow sheets of water that were refreshed by winter rains and spring floods. Settlers who needed well-drained land for fields and orchards and remembered the devastation of floods in the Mississippi Valley shunned areas like Couch's Lake and Guild's Lake in northwest Portland. Smith and Bybee Lakes in North Portland are remnants of a landscape that also covered much of the south shore of the Columbia with a maze of sloughs and marshes.

Early settlers placed a premium on three landscape features. One was the relatively well drained terraces that sloped gradually up from the rivers—a feature shared by early settlement points such as

Oregon City, Portland, Vancouver, and the outlying Portland neighborhoods of Linnton and St. Johns. A second feature was streams with enough flow and fall to generate water power for sawmills and other basic factories. Tanner Creek, which dropped out of the West Hills behind the Portland townsite, is now hidden in concrete conduits; Johnson Creek in southeast Portland still flows free. The third feature was the fertile and easily tilled prairie of the Tualatin Plains, which attracted many of the area's first farmers to what is now Washington County.

Given this early dependence on the natural landscape, it is not surprising that early Canadian and American settlers within what is now the Portland metropolitan region made decisions that resembled those of Native Americans.

The new post of the Hudson's Bay Company at Fort Vancouver soon bustled with activity under the management of John McLoughlin. The site offered convenient access to the four points of the compass — up the Columbia River to the network of interior trading posts and beaver streams, down the Columbia to the wider world, north along the Cowlitz River corridor to Puget Sound, south up the Willamette River. McLoughlin used Sauvie Island to pasture cattle to feed his trading post. By 1850 the southern end of the island would have a cluster of farmers raising livestock and potatoes.

Oregon City was a secondary center and gathering point. Beginning in 1840–41, John McLoughlin and Methodist missionaries from the United States contended for control of what seemed a natural location for a town. Located below the Willamette River falls, it was a necessary stopping point for small sailing ships and canoes. Above the falls were rich Willamette Valley plains, already settled at the "French Prairie" (Champoeg) by French-speaking employees of the Hudson's Bay Company. Oregon City was also midway between the Tualatin River from the west and the Clackamas River route to the east, along which a number of early pioneers settled. By the winter of 1842–43, the new town had thirty buildings and a gristmill. It was the first destination for a swelling overland migration that brought 800 American settlers to Oregon in 1843 and 1200 in 1844. Maps of early roads and farms clearly show its centrality as a communication center around 1850. With 933 residents, Oregon City was big enough to have a "suburb" in the form of Linn City (population 124).[11]

The most important agricultural district in the circle around Oregon City was the Tualatin Plains, the northernmost of the Willamette Valley prairies. The plains lay west of Rock Creek in what is now the Hillsboro-Forest Grove-North Plains-Banks area of Washington County. In the 1830s Hudson's Bay Company employees from Fort Vancouver sometimes drove cattle over the muddy passes of the Tualatin Mountains (West Hills) to fatten on rich summer grasses of the valley. In the 1840s American wheat farmers pushed aside the British cattle. The newcomers saw no reason to hew farms out of dense forest. Their ideal location was on the margin of the open grasslands, with easy access to timber and fresh spring water from low foothills. Early Washington County towns included Columbia (Hillsboro) and West Tualatin (Forest Grove) as the bulk of development was separated from the Willamette River by the Tualatin Mountains and their forested western slopes.

Within this early settlement system, the site of the future Portland was Oregon's first highway rest area. Native Americans and fur trappers had cleared part of a dry, sloping bank on the west side of the Willamette roughly halfway between Fort Vancouver and Oregon City. It was a good spot to cook a meal, spend a night, or repair equipment. Jesse Applegate later remembered his visit to "the clearing": "We landed on the west shore, and we went into camp on the high bank where there was little underbrush. . . . No one lived there and the place had no name; there was nothing to show that the place had ever been visited except for a small log hut near the river, and a broken mast of a ship leaning against the high bank. There were chips hewn from timber, showing that probably a new mast had been made there . . . but there was no prophet to tell of the beautiful city that was to take the place of the gloomy forest." [12]

When William Overton and Asa Lovejoy claimed the square mile that would become downtown Portland in 1844, they knew that they had a promising site. As two British spies described the new town in 1846, "the situation of Portland is superior to that of Linnton, and the back country of easier access. There are several settlements on the banks of the [Willamette] river below the falls, but the water, covering the low lands during the freshets render them valueless for cultivation, and but few situations can be found adapted for building on." [13] Their report is more useful to historians than it was to the British Foreign Office because the two nations agreed to the present Canada-U.S. border in the same year.

As the California gold rush created a booming San Francisco market for Oregon wheat and lumber, newly platted Portland struggled to establish itself as the head of oceangoing navigation on the Willamette River. "Head of navigation," of course, was a moving target. It varied with the season, the length of the wharf, the type of ship, and the foolishness of the captain.

The first rivalry was with the ambitious town of Milwaukie, founded in 1848 six miles up the Willamette from Portland. Milwaukie had the *Western Star* newspaper, which began publication two weeks before Portland's *Oregonian*. It also had the *Lot Whitcomb of Oregon*, the first steamboat built in the territory. The steamer could make 14 miles per hour on its run to Astoria during its inaugural season of 1851, but trouble was in the wings. One boat after another began to scrape bottom or bend a propeller on the Ross Island sand bar. Captain John Couch, who had relocated his business interests from Oregon City to Portland, announced that the river at Ross Island normally had only four feet of water and claimed to have ridden clear across on horseback. Milwaukie was soon a stranded town, too risky a destination for increasingly expensive steamers.

The battle between Portland and St. Helens was tougher. Thirty miles closer to the open ocean on the main stem of the Columbia, St. Helens built a road over the Cornelius Pass to the Tualatin wheat farms. Portland countered with the "Great Plank Road," the first "paved" route along the Sunset corridor. Then came the news — in February 1851 — that the Pacific Mail Steamship Company of San Francisco was going to terminate its California-Oregon service at St. Helens. The company's worry was another sandbar, this time at Swan Island. The contest hung in the balance for two years until Pacific Mail found it was unable to make full cargos at St. Helens and began to advertise direct service between San Francisco and Portland. The course of Portland's growth from these modest beginnings can be traced in Table 1 (p. 52).

After gaining control of trade between the Willamette Valley and California, Portland entrepreneurs looked eastward. Central to the city's prosperity was the Oregon Steam Navigation Company, the Portland owned company that controlled travel to eastern Oregon, Washington, and Idaho. Settlers east of the Cascades hated its monopoly and high freight charges, but Portlanders liked the jobs and money that it funneled to the city. Contemporaries called it Oregon's "millionaire-making machine."

On September 10, 1883 Portland finally celebrated its connection to the nation's transcontinental railroad system via the Northern Pacific Railroad. The line had opened for business in the summer, but the official golden spike was driven at Deer Lodge, Montana on September 8. Two days later Portland welcomed a trainload of dignitaries including former president Ulysses S. Grant. The following year the city gained a second connection to the Union Pacific system. The lines eastward through the Columbia Basin joined rail routes southward through the Willamette Valley to California, matching the region's river steamers with locomotives.

The intersection of river valley routes has continued to channel Portland's continental connections. Driving eastward up the Columbia on Interstate 84, it is common for a single glance to take in heavy trucks, barge tows, Burlington Northern trains on the north shore, and Union Pacific-Santa Fe trains on the south shore. The freight lines haul grain, wood chips, and bulk minerals for export through Portland and return with racks of Asian automobiles and containers stuffed with manufactured goods from Japan and Korea. At right angles to the Columbia corridor, I-5 runs through the Puget-Willamette Trough from Canada to California. Air traffic to San Francisco passes over the Willamette towns. Flights between Portland's Columbia-shore airport and the midcontinent hubs of Minneapolis, Chicago, and Denver take off and land parallel to the river and skirt the slopes of Mount Hood.

## REGIONAL CITY

Ask someone from Portland to describe her city. Her frequent answer is, "We're not Seattle." Hovering just out of hearing are the opening words of the phrase: "Thank God we're not . . ."

What Portlanders usually have in mind is the tone and pace of life. Seattle is frantic, congested, fast paced: New York with coffee. Portland is comfortable, low key, willing to take some time to enjoy its surroundings. Ever since it ran off with the Klondike miners, Seattle has been the "fast" town and Portland the stay-at-home sister. Downtown Seattle is a set of concrete canyons, but downtown Portland preserves the human scale of short, walkable blocks and inviting public spaces. Seattle is style conscious—think television's Frasier and Niles Crane—while Portland is proudly frumpy. Even well traveled professional athletes see the difference. "It's different from say a Seattle," said Trail Blazers point guard Greg Anthony in 1999. "There's much more of a small-town feel to it." Forward Scottie Pippen agreed: "It gives you the opportunity to be in the city, but not really feel like you're in a big city with so much to stress you out."[14] Natives of Portland drive too slow, not too fast, leaving vulgar displays of horsepower to Californians. Here's item number four in a list of "Ten Things a New Yorker Would Notice About Portland" in the local independent 'zine *Rotund World*: "Automobile drivers are polite, though completely out to lunch. They become unhinged at the blast of a horn, so that the streets are eerily absent of the fanatical screeching and din of ordinary life."[15]

Stereotypes aside, Portland and Seattle in the twentieth century *did* pursue substantially different economic goals and roles that have strongly affected their character. Downtown Seattle stands with its back to Mount Rainier and looks to Puget Sound and the Pacific—outward to Alaska, to national competitors, and to world markets. Local promoters in 1992 could issue a report entitled "International Seattle" with very little bashfulness.[16] Downtown Portland stands with its back to the West Hills and looks eastward toward Mount Hood and the Columbia River—inward to continental resources and markets. It has been a regional city in contrast to networked Seattle.

Portland's regional economy has been based on its natural advantages of location. Columbia River steamers and railroads that used the "water level" route to the interior made the young city the bustling entrepôt for the vast Columbia Basin. From the 1860s (steamers) and 1880s (railroads), they hauled in raw materials for transshipment or processing. Grain elevators, flour mills, and lumber mills came early. Lumber and grain schooners crowded the banks of the Willamette to take on cargos for California markets. Shipyards and factories to turn out cheap softwood furniture soon followed.

Expansion of the regional railroad network into the lands behind the Columbia River bluffs opened what geographer Donald Meinig called the Great Columbia Plain and what boosters called the Inland Empire. *Honey in the Horn*, while canvassing Oregon's early twentieth-century agriculture, makes a stop at an unnamed Columbia River town that is probably The Dalles, where author H. L. Davis spent some of his youth. The result is the epitome of boom times in the hinterland:

Early waterfront (Oregon Historical Society Neg. 24023). At the turn of the last century, factories, warehouses, and private wharves lined the Willamette waterfront. River steamers ran goods and people up and down the Columbia and multimasted schooners hauled Oregon lumber to California cities.

Times were livening up in the Columbia River towns that fall, because the upper country was getting not one railroad, but two, and old E. H. Harriman and James J. Hill were out letting contracts, buying rights of way, and banging out court injunctions back and forth. . . . Men were already piling into the middle river ports to be on hand when work opened, every side-hill freight station in the upper country was petitioning to be the county seat of a new county, and windows of real-estate offices were loaded with maps of Gainesville and Wilkinsburg and Petersonville, Cherry Vale and Apple Heights and Gooseberry Villas and Sweet Pea Home Sites, all right in the path of future development, and all requiring only the investment of a little small change to make a man a capitalist for life. There was a carnival on all over the streets, and deckhands and cowboys and shovel-stiffs and real-estate promoters elbowed their way around under the arc-lights with mobs of street-show pitchmen and girls on the prowl picking at their flanks. Steamboats snorted and boomed their whistles from the river, a merry-go-round tooted and wiggled its varnished ponies.[17]

The rise of a livestock industry east of the Cascades early in the new century supported the production of woolen goods (Pendleton, Jantzen, White Stag) and meat packing. When the "North Bank" railroad (now part of the Burlington Northern system) completed its Columbia River line and bridge to Portland in 1907, Swift and Company took advantage by opening a huge meat packing plant where 1500 workers processed cattle from eastern Oregon and Washington. Another dozen large factories quickly followed. Swift also built the community of Kenton to house its employees. The neighborhood business district ran along Denver Avenue, with housing for managers on one side of the avenue and housing for workers on the other. For many years the Imperial Hotel in downtown Portland was the cattlemen's hotel, with copies of eastern Oregon newspapers always ready for its guests.

World War II turned this comfortable regional trading center upside down. In the official language of federal bureaucrats who worried about the home front, it was a "congested war production area." In the accelerating pace of daily life it was a boom town, another Leadville or Virginia City with defense contracts in place of gold and silver mines.

The cause was shipbuilding. Industrialist Henry Kaiser, fresh from helping to build Boulder and Grand Coulee dams, opened the huge Oregon Shipbuilding Company north of the St. Johns neighborhood in 1941. His Swan Island and Vancouver, Washington yards went into production two months after Pearl Harbor. At the peak in 1943–44, metropolitan Portland counted 140,000 defense workers. They built more than 1000 oceangoing combat craft and Liberty ships — one of the latter in eleven days from laying the keel to launch.

War brought thousands of new faces. The Kaiser yards placed help-wanted ads in eleven states. The response almost emptied the rest of Oregon and drew the unemployed from small towns in Idaho and Montana. Chartered trains from the east coast brought other workers. Among the arrivals in 1943 and 1944 were African Ameri-

Shipyards in World War II (Oregon Historical Society Neg. 55354). Armies of welders, riveters, and fabricators at the Swan Island, North Portland, and Vancouver shipyards were simultaneously at work on dozens of Liberty ships at the height of war production. Portland's output helped to shift the balance in the "tonnage war" between German U-boats and Allied convoys in the North Atlantic and to supply far-flung American forces in the Pacific Theater.

cans from Oklahoma, Arkansas, Texas, and Louisiana. Between 1940 and 1944 the metropolitan population grew from 501,000 to 661,000. One could safely assume, in the war years, that every third person standing at the bus stop or lining up for a double feature was a newcomer.

War work could also be women's work. By the end of 1943 the Kaiser yards employed 20,500 women. One out of three filled the sorts of office jobs that were already open to women, but hundreds of others who had recently graduated from training classes at Benson Polytechnic High School worked as electricians, painters, machinists, and pipefitters. More than 5000 earned what was then an impressive $1.20 per hour as welders. "I needed to work and that was the best-paying work I could find, so naturally I took it," remembered Alice Erickson.[18] Kaiser's Women's Services Division operated childcare centers on round-the-clock shifts synchronized with shipyard work and provided takeout meals that busy wives could pick up on their way home. Patricia Cain Koehler later recalled her work as a teenage electrician who helped to build escort aircraft carriers in Vancouver, Washington.

We girls wore leather jackets, plaid flannel shirts, and jeans we bought in the boys department of Meier & Frank. It was 1943, we were eighteen years old, our first year of college was over. . . . Three local shipyards were recruiting workers from the East Coast and the South. They advertised in Portland, too: HELP WANTED: WOMEN SHIPBUILDERS. Cartoons asked, "What are you doing to help the war?" They showed women sipping tea, playing cards, and relaxing. "THIS?" And then a smiling woman worker with lunch box, her hair tied up in a scarf, a large ship in the background, "Or THIS?" . . .

Together my girlfriend and I applied to be electrician helpers at the Kaiser Vancouver Shipyards. . . . The day came . . . when we graduated to journeyman-electrician at $1.20 per hour. We celebrated by applying for jobs on the hookup crews, which worked aboard ships at the outfitting dock. I was assigned to fire control. That meant guns! My leadman had never had a female working for him, and he was skeptical. Like a shadow, I followed his every move, anticipating what tool he needed next and handing it to him before he could ask. After a few days of this he relaxed and began teaching me the ropes—or, rather, the wires. . . .

My first solo assignment was hooking up the forty-millimeter gun directors on the starboard side. . . . Occasionally I looked down into the swift current of the Columbia River and noticed small boats dragging for a worker who had fallen in. . . . Once when climbing down a ladder clogged with welding leads (large rubber hoses), I slammed a steel-toed boot against one of them and broke a toe. The doctor taped it to its neighbor and I went on working. On another occasion I broke my elbow in a fall, lost a day getting it set, and learned to work left-handed.[19]

Shipbuilding was easy come and easy go. Victory took the federal government out of the ship buying business. With surplus wartime freighters clogging private markets, there was no reason to keep the shipyards in operation. Unlike the case with aircraft production cities, the Portland boom left no added base for industrial growth. Henry Kaiser turned his attention to steel and automobiles. His legacy for Portland was not manufacturing but the pioneering Kaiser-Permanente HMO. Intended originally to keep war workers on the job, "Kaiser" now enrolls 400,000 Portland area residents.

The evaporation of shipbuilding ushered in two decades of political and economic caution. While Portland rested on its geographical advantage, arch rival Seattle took entrepreneurial risks that made it *the* city of the American Northwest. As Seattle-based Boeing developed and sold its first commercial jetliners, Seattle between 1958 and 1968 mounted a series of public initiatives that Portland was unable to match. Community efforts assured a successful world's fair, developed convention and sports facilities, revitalized its port, and enjoyed the rise of a major research university.

Portland faced similar opportunities and attempted parallel projects but failed to match Seattle's entrepreneurial spirit. Contemporary observers commented on the contrasting approaches to public business. Journalists such as Neal Morgan in *Westward Tilt* (1963) and Neal Peirce in *The Pacific States of America* (1972) and scholars such as Earl Pomeroy in *The Pacific Slope* (1965) and Dorothy Johansen in *Empire of the Columbia* (1967) all perceived different spirits of public and private enterprise. Seattle was project-centered, entrepreneurial, and expansive. Portland was process-oriented, cautious, and localized. Reasoning by analogy from the realm of individual ethics, conservative Portland tended to regard public debt as a flaw of civic character. While Seattleites built in anticipation of growing business, Portlanders judged facility needs by current demand and by the potential of purely local and regional markets. "Unlike Seattle, which is in its own promotional vocabulary a 'go-ahead' city," Johansen wrote, "Portland moved in 1965 as slowly and deliberately as it did in 1865, and there remains considerable sentiment . . . to 'keep things as they are.' " [20]

Different experiences with major expositions illustrate the contrast. The two cities began by competing not only for regional and national attention but also for the same date. Led by the Portland Chamber of Commerce, Oregonians decided in 1954 to commemorate the centennial of statehood with a celebratory exposition in Portland in 1959. Within a few months, Seattleites began to explore a fifty-year follow-up to the Alaska-Yukon-Pacific Exposition of 1909. As second in line, Seattle reluctantly ceded 1959 to Portland and shifted its target to 1961 (later 1962).

The parallels ended with the timing. The Seattle exposition grew steadily from a regional reaffirmation of the Alaska connection to "a means of recapturing prestige . . . as the gateway to the Orient" and, finally, to the global theme of "the wonders of the 'space age' science" and the future of "Century 21." [21] The promoters tapped the city for $15 million in site and building improvements, secured $7.5 million from the State of Washington, and obtained $9 million for federal participation. The federal commitment clinched designation as a world's fair by the Bureau of International Expositions. Official sanction allowed the planners to attract international exhibits and to draw on the best national expertise, ranging from the Walt Disney organization to the National Science Foundation. Reams of favorable publicity and 9,600,000 paid visits made it the most successful of all postwar American world's fairs, teaching outsiders that the Northwest's metropolis started with an "S."

Portland had preempted 1959 but mounted the Oregon Centennial Exposition on the cheap. Portland whittled its vision to the comfortable model of local "pioneer days." Despite early national publicity and a small international trade fair, the celebration had little to attract Portlanders, let alone visitors from out of state. Planned initially to use a new Portland coliseum and convention center, the exposition had to turn to the Oregon legislature when the Portland facility bogged down in neighborhood politics. The parsimonious state doled out $2.6 million in two grudging installments in 1958 and 1959, barely in time to remodel a livestock exhibition hall into display space. Portlanders themselves quickly learned to stay away from what turned out to be little more than an interminable county fair without the plum preserves and Future Farmers.

Portland was both cheap and slow in modernizing its port. Through the 1950s, Portland outpaced Seattle in general cargo movements and the bulk shipments of farm and forest products that traditionally constituted most of the trade over northwest docks. Portlanders supported new maritime facilities by voting $6.5 million for the city's Commission of Public Docks in 1954 and $9.5 million in 1960. However, the 1960 figure covered less than half the needs listed by consultants. Since the established operators in the Columbia River trade who dominated the Docks Commission agreed with outside consultants that the new technology of containerization was inappropriate for traditional regional bulk commodities, the funds finally went to improve familiar general cargo docks.

Seattle meanwhile turned to facilities for containerized cargo out of a sense of necessity. A series of consultant studies and a KING-TV documentary on "Lost Cargo" articulated a growing crisis of confidence in Port of Seattle management in 1959, setting off several years of bureaucratic infighting and contests for the elected seats on the Port Commission. Firmly in place by 1963, a new growth-oriented majority spent more than $100 million to modernize and upgrade marine terminals and industrial land as a way to bypass Portland's historic advantage and compete directly with Oakland. The Port Commission gambled on the development of long range business in which containerized cargos would move through Seattle in transit between Asia and the ports on the Atlantic. The rhetoric of the revitalized port reflected its new energy, "catapulting" to "record-breaking performance" by the mid-1960s and "barreling full bore" in its "relentless escalation" toward full success.[22]

The impact was immediate. Seattle passed Portland in the value of both import and export trade between 1967 and 1977. Portland retained its historic role as an exporter of high bulk, low value western commodities such as minerals, wood products, and farm products while gaining selected high tonnage imports such as automobiles. Seattle developed as a comprehensive international port that shipped and received extensively processed high value goods. A key step came in 1970, when the development of new container terminals convinced a consortium of six Japanese shipping lines to make Seattle their first port of call on the West Coast. In 1967 Seattle exports carried an average value of $.05 per pound compared with $.04 for Portland. The comparable figures for 1986 were $.36 for Seattle and $.08 for Portland.[23]

Expansion of the University of Washington was a final difference. After divisive internal battles over political loyalty oaths during the early 1950s, the university in 1958 hired a new president who encouraged faculty to tap the rapidly growing pool of federal research funds in medicine and the sciences. Enrollment exploded from 14,000 in 1956 to 30,000 by 1968. In 1977, Seattle occupied eighth place among all metropolitan areas in receipt of federal research and development dollars to universities and sixth place for total federal research and development funds. The university itself had changed from a regional educator to a national information producer.

In contrast, statewide institutional and community jealousies retarded the evolution of Portland State College into a major university. Portland lacked the economic multiplier from a large body of out-of-town students and from faculty research grants. It also lacked Seattle's dense network of connections within national educational and research systems. The results can be read from 1970 census data on the proportion of adults aged twenty-five or older with four or more years of college: 12.8 percent of Portlanders and 15.9 percent of Seattleites.

By the time Portland felt the equivalent of Seattle's civic energy in the 1970s (see Chapter 3), Seattle's evolution into a headquarters and network city had a ten- or twelve-year lead. The results can be summed up as the contrast between a "Northwest city" and a "networked city." Seattle increasingly participates in the long-range networks of finance, investment, tourism, and trade that link the North American and East Asian core regions of the world economy. It outranks Portland, not only in the volume and value of overseas trade, but also in number of direct overseas flights, number of foreign bank offices, amount of foreign investment, number of professional consular officers, and proportion of foreign-born residents. Seattle ended its world's fair with a new convention center, science museum, and Space Needle. Portland ended the Oregon centennial with a 31-foot effigy of Paul Bunyan at a neighborhood street corner, courtesy of the Kenton Business Club and volunteer iron workers who built an I-beam skeleton, covered it with wire mesh, and troweled on concrete skin and clothing.

Paul B. and his axe are a good reminder that Portland continues to thrive as the regional transportation hub and trading post for Oregon and much of Idaho and Washington. The interrelated complex of finance, insurance, transportation, and wholesaling accounted for 14 percent of Portland area jobs in 1994, a proportion one-third greater than in the United States as a whole. A closely related growth sector in the 1990s was high end competitive business and professional services. Most commonly, law firms and accounting offices aim at regional clients, but a few Portland service firms by the 1990s had national and international clientele: Zimmer-Gunsul-Frasca's architects, Wieden and Kennedy's advertising copy writers, and large law firms, for example. A software and multimedia complex was also coalescing at the start of the new century. Telecommunications scholar Mitchell Moss used the registered location of commercial Internet domains (.com addresses) at the end of the 1990s to assess the relative standing of eighty-five cities as Internet information centers. Portland's location quotient of 3.11 placed it a satisfying sixteenth, several steps up from earlier in the decade.[24]

The third drive wheel of Portland prosperity is now export-oriented manufacturing. The six-county metropolitan area reported 150,000 manufacturing jobs in 1996, more than Pittsburgh or Cincinnati. Of these, 45,000 were in aluminum, steel products, transportation equipment, and other metal goods; 42,000 were in manufacture of computers, electrical equipment, and instruments.[25] Nike, perhaps Portland's highest profile corporation, signs endorsement contracts in Portland but manufactures its gear overseas. Statewide, high tech employment passed timber-related employment in the mid-1990s, explaining the Portland-Salem CMSA ranking (1996) as tenth in the nation in the value of its exports ($9.2 billion).[26]

Even with through flights to Tokyo and Seoul, Portland remains a regional city in comparison to Seattle. It may rank fifth among CMSAs in the number of Web domains per capita, according to March 1999 data, but its overlay of electronics, software, and sporting goods companies has yet to alter its caution or its close ties to its region.[27] Like other American river towns—Cincinnati, Louisville, St. Louis—it is stolid and sensible. Veteran Seattle journalist David Brewster noted its reflection of the Middle West and its "contented

CHAPTER 1

sense of its own place as a middling provincial capital." Regional connections remind residents that there is plenty of money to be made the old-fashioned way. Those connections have also acted like a flywheel to smooth out economic change. At the end of the century, young Portland journalist Lizzy Caston put it in baldest form: "Portland is often shaped by ideas from the past while Seattle continually looks toward the future."[28] Seattle's NBA team, after all, is the Supersonics, a name that invokes technological innovation; Portland has the Trail Blazers, whose name recalls Lewis, Clark, and the pioneers of the overland trails.

PORTLAND'S PROVINCE

The residents of Portland cherish a sense of intimacy with their setting. The connections to the region are emotional as well as economic, deeply personal as well as corporate. The core of the Portland region is the three Oregon counties of Multnomah, Washington, and Clackamas. As is typical in the West, the counties are spacious. Together they stretch 100 miles east and west, embracing city neighborhoods and portions of National Forest Wilderness areas. Visiting in 1936, reporter Ernie Pyle noted: "All around Portland there are small rivers and green fir trees. Not far away are the mountains themselves. Nature is all around. A friend of mine, searching for the reason he loves the Northwest, finally decided that the sense of having all around him these clear, cold, tumbling streams had a great deal to do with it."[29]

Portland's Standard Metropolitan Area, first defined by the Census Bureau for 1950, included the three core counties plus Clark County, Washington, just north of the Columbia. Population of that area climbed from 704,800 in 1950 to 821,900 in 1960, 1,047,000 in 1970, and 1,242,600 in 1980, for twenty-sixth place among U.S. metropolitan areas.

The statistical definitions recognized the functional region that

| Year | City of Portland | Three-County Area | Six-County Area[a] |
|------|------------------|-------------------|--------------------|
| 1860 | 2,873 | 10,390 | 14,149 |
| 1870 | 8,293 | 21,764 | 27,639 |
| 1880 | 17,577 | 41,545 | 51,532 |
| 1890 | 46,385 | 102,089 | 131,199 |
| 1900 | 90,426 | 137,292 | 170,368 |
| 1910 | 207,214 | 277,714 | 332,734 |
| 1920 | 258,288 | 342,972 | 410,266 |
| 1930 | 301,815 | 440,498 | 527,197 |
| 1940 | 305,394 | 451,423 | 548,582 |
| 1950 | 373,628 | 619,522 | 761,280 |
| 1960 | 372,676 | 728,088 | 876,754 |
| 1970 | 379,967 | 878,676 | 1,076,133 |
| 1980 | 366,383 | 1,050,418 | 1,333,623 |
| 1990 | 437,319 | 1,174,291 | 1,515,452 |
| 2000 | 513,325 | 1,414,150 | 1,886,150 |

SOURCE: U.S. Census (1860–1990), Center for Population Research, Portland State University, and Washington Office of Financial Management (2000).

[a] Portland PMSA as of 1993.

was knit together between 1900 and 1925 by electric interurban rail-roads. At the peak of the interurban system in 1915, the suburban division of Portland Railway, Light and Power served Troutdale, Gresham, Boring, Estacada, and Oregon City. Oregon Electric, a tiny cog in James J. Hill's great railroad empire, ran one line to Beaverton, Hillsboro, and Forest Grove and a second through Tualatin and Wilsonville to Salem. The Southern Pacific served Garden Home, Beaverton, and Hillsboro before swinging south to McMinnville and Corvallis.

The five million interurban riders in 1915 represented the first integration of Washington, Multnomah, and Clackamas Counties into a single system of everyday interaction. The three counties had been tied through economic exchange since the 1850s. In the new century, the interurban trains added the possibility of easy personal trips for special occasions—shopping trips and theater excursions into the city balanced by weekend visits to rural parks and amusement centers such as Canemah in Clackamas County.

The Census Bureau in recent decades has recognized the broadening reach of Portland with expanded metropolitan area definitions. Up the Willamette Valley, the official metro area gained the grain fields and vineyards of Yamhill County after 1980. In 1993 it

Portland CMSA (Irina Sharkova, Portland State University). The eight-county Consolidated Metropolitan Statistical Area combines the Salem area with Portland and Vancouver, identifying the lower half of the Willamette Valley as an increasingly integrated economic unit.

gained Columbia County and its old rival town of St. Helens. At the same time, the census joined what was now a six-county Portland-Vancouver Primary Metropolitan Statistical Area (PMSA) with the two-county Salem PMSA to make a Portland-Salem Consolidated Metropolitan Statistical Area (CMSA). The Portland PMSA had 1,515,452 residents in 1990 and an estimated 1,886,150 in 2000. The CMSA total was an estimated 2,231,350 in 2000 (twenty-second nationally).

The functional statistical region of demographers and marketing firms is a close match to a visual region that might be seen from the crest of the West Hills (at least by an ideally positioned observer on a clear day). Frances Fuller Victor remarked on the view more than a century ago: "From the ridge west of Portland you may see five snow-peaks, two great rivers. . . . Neither the camera nor the pen is equal to the task of delineating scenes on a scale of such magnificence as are grouped around Portland-on-Wallamet." [30] To the cardinal points of the compass, mountains mark the visible boundaries of greater Portland: Mount Hood to the east, Mount St. Helens to the north, the Coast Range to the west, and Mount Jefferson to the southeast. With some stretching here and tucking there, these landmarks coincide surprisingly well with the edges of the CMSA. We can think of it as the areas that can now be reached in one and a half to two hours in the Land Rover or Subaru—roughly a seventy-five-mile radius around the original city.

Visual closeness promotes a sense of immediacy, an expectation of access, and a curiously heroic self-image. Portland is a fine market for pickups and sports utility vehicles. *Outside* magazine in 1992 ranked it the fourth best city for outdoor enthusiasts. Robin Cody writes, "even today, nature is the hero among Portlanders. Nature makes us different. . . . The eruption of Mount St. Helens gave an enormous boost to Portland's collective psyche by reminding urban frontiersmen that life out here is savage, and we are trailblazers." [31]

On their weekend outings, Portlanders pick up an unconscious understanding of the valley transect popularized early in the twentieth century by British regionalist Patrick Geddes, who argued that the way to see the complex ecology of a watershed was to cut across it from one crest to the other. To drive from the center of Portland or Salem to the Cascades is to start at river and marshes, to pass through ripening fields and forested foothills, and to arrive at trailhead parking areas that give access to mountain slopes, high meadows, scree fields, glaciers, and finally bare peaks.

Portlanders have celebrated the extent of this territory since 1982 with a 195-mile Hood to Coast Relay. Twelve-member teams of runners take turns running legs of a course that starts at Timberline Lodge on Mount Hood and follows back roads to Seaside. Runners start in the chilly mountain dawn. The fastest teams finish in seventeen or eighteen hours; others take twenty-five or thirty. One thousand teams competed in August 1998 — 12,000 runners plus thousands of volunteers and two thousand support vans. The event remains eccentric and outdoorsy even when it has gained international participants, competitive for some teams and laid back for most of the rest. It seems made for a metro area that ranks first in the nation in the proportion of population regularly doing aerobic exercise.

The proximity of the natural world is fundamental to the regional literature of the Northwest. Oregonians and Washingtonians are still finding new insights while rewriting *Giants in the Earth* and *The Octopus, The Deerslayer* and *O Pioneers*. Many of the best regional novels are about the dimensions and meaning of work in a resource economy, about confronting, using, and abusing the land. Ken Kesey's family of independent "gyppo" loggers we have already met. Portlander Stewart Holbrook delighted in tales of working men, collected by Brian Booth as *Wildmen, Wobblies and Whistle-Punks: Stewart Holbrook's Lowbrow Northwest* (1992). When not writing about the mighty Paul Bunyan, James Stevens explored work in the Northwest in *Big Jim Turner* (1948). Molly Gloss in *The Jump-Off*

Bridal Veil Lumber Company (Oregon Historical Society Neg. 44631). In the early twentieth century the Bridal Veil Lumber Company cut timber on the slopes of Larch Mountain in eastern Multnomah County, used teams of eight or ten oxen to "yard" the logs to an artificial pond, and then shot the logs by chutes and flume to a mill along the Columbia River. Located within the contemporary metropolitan area, this logging camp was part of the wage worker frontier that built Portland.

*Creek* (1989) reimagined the world of a single woman homesteading in the Oregon mountains. H. L. Davis led Clay Calvert through a procession of jobs—sheep herding, hop picking, logging, hay cutting. Craig Lesley has written in the same tradition in books like *River Song* (1990) and *The Sky Fisherman* (1995). His characters pick fruit, raft rivers, sell sporting goods to tourists, farm, fish. "I hope each page honors the working West," he inscribed in my copy.[32]

Marketing companies find Portlanders to be strongly tuned to the outdoors. The Polk Company "Lifestyle Market Analyst" puts Portland in the top 20 percent of market areas for flower gardening, natural foods, camping, hiking, photography, interest in wildlife and the environment, travel, and skiing. It falls in the bottom 20 percent for watching sports on television and subscribing to cable. Portlanders are more likely than most Americans to subscribe to outdoor activity magazines but far less likely to read about golf. They like *Organic Gardening* and woodworking magazines but not magazines for tinkerers such as *Home Mechanix* or *Family Handyman*. Portland tastes are most similar to those of smaller cities in the greater Northwest: Eugene, Medford, Eureka, Spokane, Boise, Missoula, Anchorage. There is some overlap with fast lane Seattle, but very little with San Francisco. Says an executive with SRI International, another market research firm, Portland is "the psychographic center of the West" in the same way that Baltimore is a natural test market as the psychographic center of the United States.[33]

It is no surprise that Oregonians have scored high on indicators of environmentalism over the last two decades. In the 1980s, the state ranked fifth for membership in ten environmental and wildlife organizations (National Audubon Society, Environmental Defense Fund, Wilderness Society, and the like); the Nature Conservancy is perhaps the state's most popular nonprofit.[34] The "Green Index" of the Institute for Southern Studies and similar rankings by national organizations that evaluate state environmental protection efforts and accomplishments have consistently placed Oregon near the top: sixth, first, fifth, sixth. Surveys of personal values repeatedly confirm that Oregonians place high value on environmental conservation, access to outdoors, *and* resource-based jobs.

These last results reveal an unresolved tension. The Portland region is both playground *and* workplace, as its poets and novelists know. It contains wildness — and official wilderness — to be savored. It also produces crops and trees to support rural jobs and communities. The contrast helps to divide the region's urban culture from its exurban culture (a central theme of the next chapter). It lies at the heart of regional planning and policy debates over the merits and patterns of metropolitan growth, which Chapter 3 will explore. Even recreational choices mirror the tension.

Portland's weekendland stretches another fifty miles beyond the CMSA, from the Pacific coast to the far side of the Cascades, and Portlanders tend to sort naturally into coast people and mountain people. Along the Pacific edge from Newport to the Columbia River estuary are a variety of recreational communities for different tastes: deep sea fishing out of Astoria and Newport, bay fishing at Tillamook, artsy cafes and new condos at Cannon Beach, outlet malls, motels, and beachwalking at Lincoln City and Seaside, old second homes at Gearhart. Folks from Portland head to the coast to watch whales, storms, and just plain waves. They escape 85-degree days in Portland (high summer) to enjoy temperatures that often hover in the 60s.

Mountain oriented Portlanders have their own set of options. Interlacing the Cascades are the logging roads and hiking trails of the Gifford Pinchot National Forest in Washington and the Mount Hood National Forest in Oregon. There is Columbia River windsurfing at Hood River, year-round downhill skiing on Mount Hood, fast streams for kayaking, and cross-country skiing or mountain biking on back roads and trails. The magnificent Timberline Lodge, built as a WPA project on Mount Hood, offers restored rooms and hundred-mile views across the often foggy valleys.

In these lands of many uses, nonconsumptive recreation contrasts with traditional outdoor recreation that revolves around resource harvesting. Tens of thousands of birders with binoculars contrast with Oregon's 400,000 hunters and 600,000 anglers.[35] In both coastal and Cascade mountains are deer and elk for wily hunters; along the Columbia are ducks and geese. On the night before deer season opens, pickups and RVs by the thousands stream eastward from Portland, heading over Wapanitia Pass and Santiam Pass for the ponderosa pine forests of central Oregon. Duck hunters line up to take turns in the blinds overlooking the Sauvie Island wildlife refuge. Anglers proudly endure drenching winter rains to match wits with steelhead trout in the Sandy and Clackamas Rivers.

Because so much of the Oregon and Washington backcountry is public land, and because Oregon riverbanks and ocean beaches are legally open to public access, Portlanders are accustomed to using the outdoors without intermediaries. Yuppies and hunters both expect to drive to trailheads, pull out the knapsack or rifle, and head for the high country. Northwestern Oregon has surprisingly few full package rural resorts with golf courses and organized activities.

The rise of a recreation economy carries the seeds of regional conflict. Few owners of weekend homes like to look at clearcut hillsides; few farmers like to see neighboring land bulldozed and sculpted for golf courses. Small town residents may take tourist industry jobs but deeply resent the disappearance of "family-wage" work in logging or commercial fishing. Nevertheless, the growing numbers of second-home owners, retirees, transplanted entrepreneurs, and telecommuters in the outlying sections of the Portland and Eugene weekendlands have been transforming the character of much of "rural" Oregon.

Statewide voting patterns illustrate the growing cultural reach of the metropolitan centers. Key statewide elections in the 1990s included the gubernatorial victory of liberal Democrat John Kitzhaber over conservative Republican Denny Smith in 1994 and the senatorial victory of Portland Democrat Ron Wyden over Pendleton businessman Gordon Smith in the same year. In both cases, the more liberal and city-oriented candidate took not only metropolitan Portland and the university counties of Lane and Benton but also the counties of the northern coast and several central Oregon tourist counties. The counties that rejected 1992 and 2000 measures to curtail gay rights and supported a 1998 measure to allow medical use of marijuana show a similar tolerance zone. These patterns show something quite different from a standard vision of two Oregons split neatly between urban and rural. What they suggest is the influence of a newer cosmopolitan economy gradually transforming those parts of rural Oregon within easy recreational and commuting range of Portland and Eugene.

"Greater Portland" contrasts with those parts of Oregon where the western frontier is still alive, if not well. In 1990, eleven Oregon counties reported fewer than six people per square mile. These expanses of 5000-acre wheat ranches, high desert, and patches of irrigated hay meadows are wide open spaces by anyone's book. Eight counties, coastal and interior, show a persisting tradition of frontier recklessness where the murder and suicide rate in 1993 was 1.5 times the state average.[36]

To understand what is going on as Portland begins the twenty-first century, think of the Northwest as a region where two sorts of regional economy and regional identity are layered one on top of the other. The question is not whether a particular community is frontier West or new West, rural Oregon or big-city Oregon, but how it is balanced between older and newer roles in the world economy.

The engines of change are metropolitan economies. Portland, Seattle, and Eugene recruit new workers from California, Korea, and sagging software companies around Boston's Route 128. The cities need the rest of the Northwest for recreation and refreshment as much as for resources and markets. It is metropolitan Seattle that created a North Cascades National Park and metropolitan Portland that created a Columbia River Gorge National Scenic Area. Artsy ex-urbanites move to Joseph, Oregon to interact tensely with ranchers and loggers. Next door to the Roundup Room on the main street of Condon, Oregon, population 835, they can find espresso, veggie sandwiches, and a branch of Portland's biggest bookstore—after nearly three hours driving into the dry country.

For an illustration of the interweaving of the two "Northwests," stand on the Columbia River dike east of the Portland Airport. The old economy is all around you. In the distance you can see plumes of smoke from the paper mills at Camas, Washington. Plowing downriver comes a barge tow full of wood chips headed toward Portland harbor. Across the river is a long Burlington Northern train with cars full of wheat for transshipment to world markets out of Portland or

Kalama, Washington. But the new economy is equally present. You can hear the traffic humming across the Glenn Jackson Bridge on I-205. Some of the cars are carrying people from Olympia who find it easier to fly out of Portland than Seattle-Tacoma. Along the bike path come bevies of Portland information workers stretching their muscles as well as their minds on our imaginary weekend. Overhead (and overheard) are the rapid-fire landings and takeoffs of airplanes on the lucrative north-south routes served by Alaska, Shuttle by United, Horizon, and Southwest.

The dividing lines between Portland and its province are not as clear as the crest of the Cascades or the canyon of the Deschutes River. Instead, two economies and associated expectations exist side by side throughout the state. We're already living with each other, interlocked in edgy and dynamic balance and testing the possibilities of peaceful coexistence. Indeed, the central theme of the next chapter is the interaction of old and new livelihoods and ways of life within the metropolitan region itself.

RIVERSCAPE AND CITYSCAPE

The coast is impressive, the mountains inspiring, and Willamette Valley hills comforting, but rivers are still central to Portlanders' understanding of their place. Rivers furnish icons and imagery—blue herons, Forecourt Fountain, dragon boat races for Rose Festival. Undeveloped riverside land becomes cherished open space. The groomed lawns of Waterfront Park are the venue for food festivals and community celebrations. Bird watchers seek out natural places inside the urbanized area such as Oaks Bottom, Bybee Lake, or Sauvie Island. Every April weekend, thousands of fishermen follow the tradition of clogging the river below Willamette Falls with hoglines of closely linked boats to catch spring chinook salmon. Artist Dennis Cunningham has captured some of the attachment in lino-

"Willamette White Sturgeon" (Dennis Cunningham, linocut, 1986, Visual Chronicle of Portland). Dennis Cunningham's linocut celebrates the close connection between Portlanders and their river, locating its fishermen along the Willamette near Oaks Bottom, south of downtown and Ross Island.

cut prints such as "Sauvie Island" and "Willamette White Sturgeon" that surround stylized views of the river with symbols and maps of the region.

Every city has its list of must-see sites and sights. These are the stops on Grey Line tours, the places to take visiting relatives, the views that make it onto postcards. In Portland the list is heavily tinged with green and blue: Rose Test Garden, Crystal Springs Rhododendron Garden, Japanese Garden, Pittock mansion with views over the green city, Multnomah Falls in the Columbia Gorge. The most frequent postcard scene remains Mount Hood from the Rose

Garden, although pesky trees are slowly blocking the view. Closing fast is downtown Portland from the east bank of the Willamette. The background is darkly forested hills, the foreground a blue-green river. Between are a set of buildings that rise to a central peak as an ensemble. Only one corporate tower stands out, and that cloaked in tasteful salmon-colored glass.

Writers also foreground the riverscape. Speaking at a 1998 gathering to consider the future of Johnson Creek (which closely parallels the Portland/Clackamas County line before reaching the Willamette), David James Duncan described a childhood "falling in love with every creek and river I saw" as his family moved around Portland's eastern suburbs. If you pay attention to rivers, he said, "you grow happily haunted by the sound of English words *riffle, rise, rain,* the Indian words *Clackamas, Chewana, Celilo, Wallawalla,* the primordial Greek word *logos* coupled with the sound of primordial water purling over equally primordial stone." [37] In Ursula LeGuin's science-fiction novel *The Lathe of Heaven* (1971), sudden changes in the configuration of Willamette bridges tell the protagonist when he has shifted to a parallel universe.[38] In a text and photography collaboration with photographer Roger Dorland about the cityscape of Northwest Portland (*Blue Moon over Thurman Street,* 1993), she draws an explicit comparison of natural human flows:

**Street like a riverbed**
**lives like a river**
  **busy noisy**
  **on the run**
  **going on going**
**downstream** [39]

The typical postcard correctly highlights downtown as the largest single concentration of Portland area jobs: 108,000 in 1995 and still growing in defiance of a common urban trend. Downtown in turn is part of a vast riverside employment corridor. Within one mile of the Willamette River in Multnomah, Washington, and Clackamas counties are found 214,000 jobs, or 39 percent of all employment in the three counties.[40] Because of the strength of downtown and the port, the river corridor houses half the tri-county jobs in finance, insurance, real estate, transportation, and public utilities.

In this way, Portland preserves the economic geography of the nineteenth century. In the "first Portland" rail and water transportation created an industrial/working class corridor that coalesced as the south-north axis of the city in the 1870s and 1880s. Fulton (now the Terwilliger neighborhood) anchored the corridor on the west bank of the Willamette. North of Fulton's factories and worker housing was South Portland, the city's best remembered immigrant neighborhood with Italian groceries and Italian fraternal organizations, Jewish schools and synagogues. Then came waterfront docks and warehouses that were interspersed with the cheap lodgings of skid road. The wharves and mills of the industrial waterfront resumed north of the growing rail yards, while workers filled the small adjacent houses of Slabtown. Further downriver, the waterfront settlement of Linnton developed a cluster of wood products factories.

The east side of the river developed as part of the same industrial corridor. East Portland and Albina were the Hoboken and Jersey City of the Willamette — industrial suburbs built around docks, mills, factories, and railroad yards. They were tough communities of saloons and boarding houses, trainmen and Irish immigrants. East Portland, set behind a marshy waterfront directly across the river from Portland, was platted in 1861 and incorporated in 1870. Its legal boundaries stretched from Southeast Holgate to Northeast Halsey. To the north was Albina, laid out in 1873 and incorporated in 1887. Because the transcontinental and California railroads first linked up in Albina, the east side city assumed a central economic role as a railroad switching and repair center managed by the Northern Pacific Terminal Company and then the Union Pacific (after 1890). Up to a thousand rail cars rolled in and out of Portland on a busy day. The Pacific Coast Elevator, whose million-bushel capacity was unrivaled west of the Twin Cities, could unload grain from eight rail cars and load it into two ships at the same time. Planing mills, lumber yards, sash-and-door factories, and other manufacturing plants filled in Albina's industrial roster. Boarding houses and small cottages climbed the bluff behind the factories. The surviving symbol of this first industrial era is the Union Pacific smokestack, built in 1887 on "a foundation that would last for all time."

Industrial growth and the first Willamette River bridges (1887, 1889, 1891, 1894) paved the way for the Great Consolidation of 1891—the merger of Portland, East Portland, and Albina into a single supercity. Just as they do today, Portlanders a century ago kept a wary eye on upstart Seattle. When the 1890 census showed that Seattle was crowding toward the title of second largest city on the west coast (after San Francisco), Portland boosters swung into action. The newly founded Chamber of Commerce pushed a referendum on consolidation. East siders, they argued, would benefit from the removal of bridge tolls. West side businesses would gain expanded markets. Voters agreed. Consolidation instantly boosted the area of Portland from 7 square miles to 26 square miles. Two years later the city grew another 50 percent by annexing chunks of the southwest hills, Sellwood, and all the east side as far out as 24th Street.

The waterfront in the early twentieth century was skid road, factories, and immigrant neighborhoods, and it hosted some of Portland's most bitter labor-management battles. In 1922, dock workers walked out and lost, leaving the waterfront in the control of shipping companies. Eleven years later, the International Longshoremen's Association organized a single local for the entire coast and went out on strike in May 1934. Over the summer the strike idled 3000 Portland waterfront workers and 15,000 trade-dependent workers.

At first the police allowed pickets to run off strike breakers and even to cut loose one ship that drifted into the Broadway Bridge. The demands of the business community soon caused Mayor Joseph Carson to change his orders and enlist the police on the side of the companies. Senator Robert Wagner of New York, in town as an advance man for Franklin Roosevelt's planned visit to the new Bonneville Dam, was the target of shots from company guards when he tried to visit the docks. The incident, plus the threat of holding up Bonneville, gave Wagner leverage to force the employers into arbitration—a tacit legitimation of the ILA.

Portlanders were busy manipulating the natural riverscape to make new industrial land. Dredge spoils and fill extended the Willamette River shoreline in areas like the mouth of Sullivan's Gulch, the route of present I-84, turning wetlands into buildable real estate. Southeast Union Avenue (now Martin Luther King, Jr. Boulevard) originally ran on pilings over mud flats before much of the Central Eastside Industrial District was developed on made land. The Northern Pacific filled Couch's Lake for rail yards now being converted to housing of the River District. Organizers of the Lewis and Clark Exposition (see Chapter 3) distributed exhibition halls around the backwater of Guild's Lake in Northwest Portland, keeping it clean by pumping in fresh river water from the Willamette. The end of the fair began the long process of filling the lake for industrial land. Much of the soil on which the Guild's Lake industrial district is built was washed down from the West Hills. High pressure hoses carved the streets and lots of Westover Terrace out of the hills, and wooden flumes carried the suspended dirt into the shallow lake. By the mid-1910s the first houses speckled the bare hillside. Guild's Lake itself was a drying and settling mud flat by the 1930s, awaiting development during World War II.

Port of Portland dredges had already straightened the Willamette River at Swan Island. The port shifted the channel from the east side of the island to the west and attached the island itself to the east bank, readying another tract first for an airport and then for massive industrialization after 1940. The renewal of Portland as an international port in the 1970s and 1980s continued land use trends first identified in the 1910s. Modern ports are great consumers of land, especially for container yards and automobile processing. Wheat is still loaded from two elevators opposite downtown, but most port functions have moved steadily downstream and onto the Columbia River—to Terminal 4, Terminal 6 and Rivergate, the Port of Vancouver, and perhaps in the future to Hayden Island. Arriving are containers stuffed with Asian manufactures, plus plenty of Hondas, Toyotas, Hyundais (an average of 280,000 per year in the 1990s). Grain, wood chips, and soda ash go out. The new longshoremen make their living operating the controls of huge container cranes. Federal dredges keep the 100-mile Columbia River channel open to the sea at 40 feet (compared to Seattle's 45-foot access to open ocean).

Even as it continues to be Portland's economic artery, the Willamette is far cleaner than a generation ago. In 1962 newscaster Tom McCall vaulted to statewide prominence and eventually the state house with a documentary on "Pollution in Paradise." City sewage, farm runoff, and organic waste from pulp mills and canneries had arrogated the river's oxygen, killed aquatic life, and created huge summertime sludge rafts. Cleanup that started in the mid-1960s brought the river back to life by 1980. As a next step, the city of Portland has since 1991 been involved in a thirty-year, $800 million project to separate storm drainage from waste water. Meanwhile, industrial contamination of bottom sediments and shoreline led to a Superfund designation for the lower five miles of the Portland Harbor in 2000.

Rivers are also political and social divides. The political difference between the north and south sides of the Columbia—between Washington and Oregon—we can save for Chapter 3. Even in the heart of the city, however, common wisdom in the 1990s defined not

"Bon Voyage" (Andrew Haley, charcoal, 1996, Visual Chronicle of Portland). Andrew Haley's charcoal drawing depicts the grain and bulk cargo ships that still call at Willamette River docks and elevators within sight of downtown. Ungainly container ships and waddling auto carriers call downstream at the Port of Portland's Terminal 4 on the Willamette and Terminal 6 on the Columbia.

one but two Portlands, divided by the Willamette. In popular under-standing, eastside was long eastside, westside was westside, and the twain met only at Blazer games. Local politics have often been stated in terms of west side "haves" and east side "have-nots." In local imagery, as journalist Keith Moerer pointed out, east siders characterized the west side as "rich; snooty; where the city's fat cats live and work; where status seekers begin their climb."[41] West siders have believed in contrast that the east side was poor, flat, dull, and dangerous. The west side waterfront has a park, the east side a freeway (and in 2000, a floating walkway). There are far more stock brokers at work west of the Willamette, more RV dealers and bowling alleys on the east. Restaurant entrepreneur Bill McCormick expressed the common understanding in the early 1980s when he

CHAPTER 1

chose the west side suburbs for a new establishment: "Now don't get me wrong.... It's just that, when it came time to choose a spot for the restaurant, we felt more comfortable in Beaverton. You can take a square mile in Beaverton and come pretty close to the demographics. East Portland has some magnificent residential neighborhoods, but it's a checkerboard ... you never know who's going to be living two blocks on either side of you." [42]

Census data have also supported popular wisdom. Comparing east side and west side census tracts on accepted indicators of social and economic status such as years of education, income, and professional-managerial employment shows that west side census tracts have been consistently higher, with a gap that has grown since 1950. Within the suburban ring there is a consistent gradation from higher status and west side Washington County to middle status Clackamas County spanning the river and to lower status Clark County across the state border (Table 2).

The social balance tilted again in the 1990s as the east side got hip. The median housing price in the Portland metro area rose 68 percent from 1990 to 1998—the result of economic boom and in-

TABLE TWO   Social and Economic Indicators, 1990

|  | Washington County | Clackamas County | Clark County, Washington |
|---|---|---|---|
| Percent of residents with B.A. or equivalent | 30 | 24 | 17 |
| Percent of workers with executive, administrative, managerial, or professional jobs | 32 | 28 | 24 |
| Household income (median) | $35,554 | $35,419 | $31,800 |

migration hitting a depressed and underbuilt market from the 1980s. Increases hit the west side and Washington County first, creating a imbalance in prices that drew buyers to the more affordable east side. Stable neighborhoods like Irvington or Alameda felt the price increases in the early 1990s; lower status neighborhoods like Kerns and Eliot felt the change in the later 1990s. In a sense, this is the return of the third generation. Grandparents settled down in a new Dutch colonial or bungalow in the mid-1920s, for example. Their children graduated from east side high schools but returned from college to buy new houses in the Southwest Hills or Beaverton in the 1960s. Their grandchildren in the 1990s returned to now stylish bungalows and supported trendy shops and restaurants scarcely dreamed of fifteen years earlier.

Rivers are economic spines and social divides, but they are also threats and challenges. They flood when warm rains melt snowpack and pour off saturated fields. High water in 1894 inundated much of downtown and helped to push the central business district toward higher ground along Fifth, Sixth, and Broadway. A near repeat in February 1996 brought out civic spirit when volunteers pitched in to raise the downtown seawall with a wood and sandbag parapet.

The most socially disruptive flood came on May 30, 1948. Swollen by weeks of heavy rain, the Columbia River at Portland crested fifteen feet higher than its flood plain, held back only by dikes. At 4:17 P.M. the water breached a railroad embankment that protected the wartime housing project of Vanport. While water filled sloughs and low spots, the community's 18,500 residents (down from 42,000 in 1944) had 35 minutes to escape. The rising water tumbled automobiles and swirled Vanport's wooden apartment buildings off their foundations like toy boats. Only fifteen residents died in the Memorial Day flood, but the refugees crowded a city that was still recovering from the war and would really have preferred the Vanporters to have evaporated (Mayor Earl Riley called the place a "great headache"). Part of the problem was race. More than 1000 of the flooded

Vanport flood (Oregon Historical Society Neg. 68883). On Memorial Day, 1948 rising waters of the Columbia River breached a railroad embankment and destroyed the six-year-old community of Vanport. Built for shipyard workers and housing more than 40,000 people at its peak in 1944, Vanport had remained an important housing option for African Americans, whom the flood forced into the already crowded Albina district.

families were African Americans, who could find housing only in the growing ghetto in North Portland. The flood has been remembered by white Portlanders as an exciting challenge and as good riddance to a prefab slum. Black Portlanders such as muralist Isaka Shamsud-Din remember it as a community disaster.

The most recent challenge calls into question Portland's ability simultaneously to use and enjoy its rivers, to capture their economic benefit *and* their emotive value. On March 11, 1998 the National Marine Fisheries Service invoked the Endangered Species Act to declare that Lower Columbia River winter steelhead trout are a threatened species. An anadromous fish like salmon, steelhead are born in flowing fresh water, migrate to the ocean, and return to spawn in fresh water. The listing covers the Columbia as far inland as Hood

River, major tributaries such as the Lewis, Sandy, and Willamette, and their smaller tributaries. A year later, March 16, 1999, the federal agency listed four more threatened populations of metropolitan fish: steelhead and chinook salmon on the upper Willamette River above Oregon City, and lower Columbia chum and chinook salmon. The upper Willamette runs use Washington County's Tualatin River, among others; the lower Columbia runs use Johnson Creek, Tryon Creek, Fanno Creek, and other very urban streams.

The listing alters the ways Portland can grow. Metro, the regional land use planning agency, has issued new guidelines for protecting streams from development. New construction must be set back 50 to 200 feet from streams (rather than the previous 25 feet), depending on land slope and the character of the waterway; the rules remove several thousand acres from the stock of developable land. Electronics firms in Washington County will need to reduce the temperature of process water before they return it to streams. Portland General Electric Company in May 1999 agreed to remove two small hydropower dams on the Sandy and Little Sandy rivers. The City of Portland, which draws its water from the Bull Run River on the northwest side of Mount Hood, will have to maintain year-round flow from its reservoir and rely more heavily on ground water. Fishermen on the Willamette have had to cut their take of spring chinook in order to protect the few wild fish mixed among hatchery fish.

Hovering in the background is the far larger problem of protecting wild salmon on the upper Columbia and Snake rivers. The Bonneville Power Administration and U.S. Army Corps of Engineers spend tens of millions of dollars each year in mitigating the effects of the region's vast system of mainstem dams for power, navigation, and irrigation. Fish are competing for water with high value farming, electricity-hungry aluminum factories, all-electric homes, and barge transportation. The region has now thought about the unthinkable—the benefits and costs of breaching four dams on the lower Snake River to allow free passage of salmon at the expense of 1200 megawatts of electrical generating capacity and 140 miles of navigable waterway.[43]

It was basic community values as well as the Endangered Species Act that prompted the 1998 "Central City Summit" to define "a healthy river that centers our community" as one of the two highest priorities for the future of central Portland. A gathering of hundreds of downtown Portland movers and shakers and idea people, the Summit agreed that the Willamette River "should be more fully embraced as the center and essence of downtown." The participants noted that the Willamette River is not only a critical ecosystem and habitat, but also a "transportation way, a playground, a theater, and a scenic resource. . . . The river is our heritage and out legacy." Writer Kim Stafford tried to sum up the relationship:

Light on the water,
salmon in the city,
bridges up,
ships from far away.

Our river is the only open space
that comes from the mountains
and holds the sunset pure.[44]

# Everyday Portlands

## RAMONA  QUIMBY'S  PORTLAND: THE  NICEST  CITY  POSSIBLE?

The 1950s that I remember from my grade school years in Dayton, Ohio are alive and well in Portland. Kids walk to school and the branch library; neighborhood movie theaters show double features suitable for families; hardware stores, groceries, and florist shops still line old commercial streets. This is the city whose downtown and older neighborhoods remind many observers of a miniature Toronto.

It is also the city of Henry Huggins, Ramona Quimby, and their friends on Klickitat Street and Tillamook Street. Henry and Ramona are the creations of Beverly Cleary. In fifteen children's books published from 1950 (*Henry Huggins*) to 1984 (*Ramona Forever*), Cleary revisited the neighborhood of her childhood in Northeast Portland. With sales topping ten million copies, the books are almost certainly the most widely circulated representation of the city. In telling her stories about Henry, Ramona, Ramona's older sister Beezus (Beatrice, actually), and their classmates, Cleary recreated a neighborhood of everyday events. Its landmarks are defined by daily activities—schools, parks, houses with friendly dogs and unfriendly dogs, churches, stores. It is an everyday world in which kids act up, fathers lose jobs, moms go to work (a change from the earlier to the later books), teachers just don't understand, and older kids call you Ramona the Pest.

It happens that I live on a very real Klickitat Street in an almost-square white house that might have belonged to the Huggins family. We can map Cleary's fictionalized cityscape onto Northeast Portland as easily as we can map John Updike's industrial city of Brewer onto Reading, Pennsylvania or William Faulkner's Yoknapatawpha County onto Lafayette County, Mississippi. Portlanders will recognize that Ramona's Rosemont and Glenwood schools are Beaumont and Fernwood middle schools. I know exactly the hill down which Henry hopes to coast on the Flexible Flyer he expects for Christmas. Grant Park is where the kids search for night crawlers. Westminster Presbyterian Church is where Ramona played a sheep in the Christmas pageant. I can find several candidates for the tan stucco and gray shingle houses Ramona passes when she tries a new route between home and first grade and meets the scary dog that steals her shoe.

Beverly Cleary's books picture a uniformly middle class city of small business owners, skilled union members, office workers, and professionals. Here her depiction is still accurate, for the Portland area is well homogenized in terms of economic class. The business strength of the central city and the slow development of suburbs has damped the class dimension of city-county politics. The income disparity between city and suburban households is less in Portland than in most metropolitan areas of comparable size (1–2.5 million).[1]

Economic classes also intermix at a relatively fine grain at the neighborhood level. Stable pockets of high income housing flourish adjacent to a variety of middle and working class districts. Portland has fewer and less concentrated poor people than most cities. Within the boundaries of the fifty largest U.S. cities in 1989, 27 percent of all children lived in poverty—nearly two-thirds of them in poor, economically distressed neighborhoods. In Portland, 18 percent of children lived in poverty—with less than a quarter in distressed neighborhoods.[2]

Despite the ease of mapping Ramona's streets and parks onto everyday Portland, we do need to add one new subtext to Cleary's homogeneous city. Her characters are white people who interact with other white people. None are even identifiably ethnic, for names like Huggins and Tebbitts are carefully Waspy.

Today the Quimby family's neighborhood remains comfortably middle class, but it is a mix of white and black, the result of a cycle of neighborhood change and revitalization between 1960 and 1990. Near to the northwest are not only African American districts but a settlement of Ethiopian immigrants. Just to the north are Mexican taquerias on Alberta Street and a Latino community development corporation in Parkrose. Vietnamese businesses line Sandy Boulevard, where an old Roman Catholic church and school have become the Southeast Asian Vicarate with 6000 parishioners.

The contrast tells us something about the balance of continuity and change in Portland. Even in the 1990s, it remained a magnet for white migrants from the northern Rockies and plains. People who tired of North Dakota winters in the 1920s escaped most easily on the Northern Pacific or Great Northern Railroad to Minneapolis, Seattle, or Portland. Interstate highways follow the same east-west grain. In the 1990s Portland was a refuge for white Californians who cashed their real estate equity and moved to a more racially homogeneous place. Among the thirty-eight metropolitan areas with populations greater than one million in 1990, only Minneapolis-St. Paul had a smaller proportion of minority residents.

At the same time, contemporary Portland has more racial variety than since the early decades of the twentieth century. Hispanic and Asian population grew rapidly in the 1980s and 1990s, with the largest percentage gains in Clackamas and Washington counties. In 1990 minorities made up 15 percent of Multnomah County, 10 percent of Washington County, and 5 percent of Clackamas County. The western suburbs of Washington County will likely pass Multnomah County in ethnic and racial diversity before 2010.

As the suburbanization of minorities suggests, foreign-born Portlanders are distributed relatively evenly across the metropolitan area. In 1990 they constituted 7 percent of the population of Multnomah and Washington Counties, 5 percent of Yamhill County, and 4 percent of Clackamas and Clark Counties. In 1998–99 there were 4700 students with limited English in Portland schools, 3300 in the larger districts of eastern Multnomah County, and 5300 in larger Washington County districts. Although small by Los Angeles standards, there is a Little Korea in Beaverton, Little Mexico in outer Washington County, Little Vietnam in east Portland, and Little Russia in Clark County.

If we look more closely at change and continuity in Portland's demography and culture, we can distinguish at least four "Portlands." Progressive Portland, Albina, the Silicon Suburbs, and the Metropolitan Borderlands are sets of neighborhoods whose residents share some distinctive political values, opportunities, behavioral expectations, and definitions of the good community. The pattern is the result of historical layering and of self-selection in residential location. Different parts of the metropolitan region are dominated by and express different sets of social and cultural values. Residents in each of the four "Portlands" like different things in their neighborhoods and prefer different packages of public services. These shared values and hopes for the future derive in part from race and ethnicity, in part from sociopolitical or ideological commitments that transcend location, and in part from the industries on which different households depend. By this latter point I mean not their class position per se, but their connections to locally rooted or nationally networked enterprise. In a sense, this is the classic sociological dichotomy of locals and cosmopolitans as experienced in the real life of a specific metropolitan area.

These cultural and economic differences are manifested in cityscapes that express different views of the city region—different ideas about what it can and should offer as a place to work and live. This chapter explores how personal values and industrial affiliations have created communities of interest. It tries to understand how such communities locate in space and utilize place. We can call the topic "social environment" or "cultural ecology" (with a bow to Rayner Banham's evocative description of the four "ecologies" of Los Angeles).[3]

## PROGRESSIVE PORTLAND

Barbara Roberts loves her neighborhood. When she returned to Portland from Boston in 1998, she picked a modest Dutch Colonial in southeast Portland's Westmoreland neighborhood. Built in 1911, the house is tucked onto a 5000-square-foot lot. There is stained glass in the front door and wicker furniture on the wide porch. A long established commercial street is only three blocks away. Roberts can walk to the grocery, the hardware store, a movie theater, and a choice of banks and restaurants, although the drug store and dime store closed soon after she moved in.

Barbara Roberts is a noteworthy representative of what I call progressive Portland—a set of people and neighborhoods that are characterized by civic activism. She entered civic life in 1969 as an advocate for handicapped children and schools. Politics was next, leading her to the Multnomah County Commission, to the state legislature, to statewide office as Oregon Secretary of State, and to the governor's office and mansion in Salem from 1991 through 1994. She worked for three years as a program executive with Harvard University's Kennedy School of Government before moving back to Portland to settle in Westmoreland, write, and run a similar program at Portland State University.

Roberts returned home because she wanted "to feel connected." Boston was "intellectually stimulating, socially stifling." In Port-

land's Sellwood-Westmoreland district she found a small town ambience that reminded her of Sheridan, the Oregon town where she
grew up. Westmoreland, she says, "feels like a neighborhood should
feel," with a mix of elderly, young couples, and children. Residents
are politically active, with high voter registration and turnout. They
notice what others do with their yards and gardens; when she took
down an aging tree that threatened her house and her neighbor,
*everyone* had a comment. People in the neighborhood restaurant/
bar treat her as family, shooing away belligerent customers who
want to upbraid her for her mistakes in Salem (she backed a deeply
unpopular sales tax to fund state services).[4]

Progressive Portland is both a place and a state of mind. Its
ideological center is still moored to John Kennedy's inaugural challenge to place public service over individual gain. It covers many
of the east side areas built up in 1870–1940 and consciously conserved since 1965, including Governor Roberts's neighborhood and
Ramona Quimby's neighborhood. It also extends to the West Hills
and close-in west side suburbs such as Beaverton, Tualatin, and
Lake Oswego. It is a land of white Americans that maps closely with
the distribution of high education levels. It has a wide range of family
income but a shared sense of civic responsibility.

Mixed together in these neighborhoods are the groups that Oregon opinion poller Adam Davis calls socially concerned liberals and
contented social moderates.[5] The former think that Oregon is performing well, but they support stronger environmental protection
and back social services for those not doing well in life. The latter
are successful, like where Oregon is going, and sympathize with environmental issues, but they hold mixed views on government programs. Together, these folks are "progressive" in pushing Portland
into the national lead on many aspects of urban planning and development, doing things that other cities imitate. Unifying issues
are compact growth, environmental protection, good public schools,
and the pleasures of a downtown that escaped modernist rework-

ing. They are also Progressives—or neo-Progressives—in the historical meaning of a political movement aimed at combining democracy and efficiency. The economic base is an alliance of downtown business and real estate interests with professional and managerial support workers (e.g., college professors) to define and pursue a public interest through rational analysis.

Progressive Portland spans partisan allegiances, as did the progressivism of Theodore Roosevelt and Woodrow Wilson. Barbara Roberts is a Liberal Democrat in capital letters. She can speak as eloquently as Eleanor Roosevelt or Lyndon Johnson about the responsibility and capacity of government to extend the blessings of liberty to the poor, the sick, the poorly educated. But Oregon is also one of the last habitats of Dwight Eisenhower's Modern Republicanism. Republican Tom McCall, governor from 1967 to 1974, we will meet in the next chapter. He lived in Portland's upper income West Hills and led a crusade for environmental protection. Victor Atiyeh, Republican governor from 1979 through 1986, looked much more conservative in the Oregon context, but still moderate in a Reaganite nation. A downtown retailer who represented the older suburbs of Washington County in the legislature for twenty years before winning state office, he and his wife live in the house they bought in the 1950s. A fiscal conservative and social moderate who saw few needs for change, he also represents the other wing of Portland's political establishment—Rockefeller Republicanism but not Gingrich radicalism.

Portland mainstream progressives believe that government provides valuable services and trust Oregon's "good government" ethos to see that it works in the public interest. In 1996, for example, they dominated the neighborhoods whose residents voted to tax themselves for light rail construction and zoo improvements. The same neighborhoods voted against Measure 47, a property tax limitation measure that passed statewide in the same year.[6]

They trust government because they *are* government. Portland area politics is open to broad participation. Weak political parties, nonpartisan city and county elections, and an absence of ethnic block voting mean that elections are fought on issues and personalities. Candidates raise their own money, assemble their own cadres of campaign workers, and try to get the most impressive array of individual endorsers to list on their letterhead. Citizen activists can emerge as successful politicians, and citizen advisory committees are important sources of ideas for public action. In a self-fulfilled evaluation, the activists of progressive Portland characterize government as open, honest, and accessible. Alert citizens believe that their input counts, that newcomers are listened to. In the description of political analyst David Broder, Portland politics are "open, unpredictable, participatory. Portland is a big city but politics seem small town. Everyone seems to know everyone else, at least the political activists do, and there is a good deal of camaraderie and tolerance."[7]

Broder's traits show in Portland's openness to leadership by women. In 1993–94, for example, women served at the same time as governor, mayor of Portland, chair of the Multnomah County Commission, and Metro executive director. David Sugarman and Murray Straus in 1988 ranked Oregon first among all states in equality for women, utilizing several indicators each for economic equality (fourth in the nation), political equality (fourth), and legal equality (first). The Institute for Women's Policy Research in 1998 found Oregon in the top quartile among states for political participation and representation, economic autonomy, and reproductive rights.[8]

The private economy is also hospitable to women. Metropolitan Portland has slightly led the rest of the country in the proportion of adult women who work, moving from 44 percent in 1970 to 62 percent in 1996 (compared with a nationwide increase from 42 percent to 59 percent). The proportion of women in professional and managerial jobs is high, and the metropolitan area is tied for third in the proportion of business firms owned by women. Indeed, the number of woman-owned businesses increased 121 percent from 1987 to 1996, the fastest growth in any metropolitan area.[9]

One subspecies among the progressives are "uptowners" from the affluent neighborhoods of the West Hills, a long crescent of expensive housing draped across a steep ridge west of downtown. In the early days of Portland, social status increased with distance from the river on the west side. The early homes of the well-to-do could be found around the Park Blocks and on Broadway, high enough for householders to enjoy views of Mount Hood from their front windows. By the early 1880s, however, tycoons began to create Portland's own "Nob Hill" in imitation of San Francisco. The mansion rows were Northwest 18th 19th, 20th, and 21st Streets—roughly the same distance from downtown Portland as Denver's Capitol Hill is from that city's center. Horse car lines followed the new houses and made for an easy commute to riverside offices. *Oregonian* editor Harvey Scott described the emerging elite neighborhood in 1890:

One is led rapidly on by the sight of grand and imposing residences in the distance, of costly structure and splendid ornamentation. Many of these are set upon whole blocks, beautifully supplied with trees, turf, and flowers, and supplied with tasteful drive-ways. . . . Among those of the spacious and magnificent West End are houses costing about $20,000 to $50,000—some of them $90,000 each—of three and four stories, and mainly in the Queen Anne style. It is upon the swell of the plateau that these fine houses begin to appear, and the views from their upper windows and turrets are extensive. . . . the region is, by popular consent—and still more by prevailing prices—forever dedicated to dwellings of wealth and beauty.[10]

The advent of family automobiles opened the steep slopes to the west to residential development. By the 1920s the West Hills were Portland's new elite district. For three generations the affluent highlanders of King's Heights, Arlington Heights, Willamette

Heights, Portland Heights, and Council Crest have enjoyed views of Mount Hood and ten-minute commutes to downtown offices. Separated by elevation from the lower income residents of the downtown fringe, successful businessmen, ambitious professionals, and monied families have been able to maintain social status and leafy living without needing to flee to suburbia.

These are Portland's mini-Brahmins. They include the heirs of old money from real estate, banking, transportation, and manufacturing, plus the successful practitioners of law, medicine, and business services. There is some big new money in Portland from growth industries such as running shoes, motels, and video stores, but this is no high roller culture. The people who get invited onto boards and commissions are those who have adopted Portland's style of conspicuous underconsumption. Perhaps the attitude reflects the New England roots of Portland's mercantile leadership in the previous century, or perhaps the difficulty of showing off mansions nested in ravines and greenery. Frances Fuller Victor observed the same pattern in the city's first century, commenting on the "snug and home-like appearance of the city" and streets that were too narrow "for the display of the fine structures already erected or in progress." [11] With their homes often muffled in morning mist and fog from November to February, these cloud people tend investments rather than rollicking on Rodeo Drive. Many are the sort of moderate Republicans who made Oregon one of the very few western states where Nelson Rockefeller ran ahead of Barry Goldwater in 1964. They are tasteful in personal style, committed and conservative in support of the arts, contented with the basic character of their community, and open to moderate social change. Readers familiar with Philadelphia might think of parts of the West Hills as an extended Chestnut Hill without the dress code.

In the case of the West Hills, proximity breeds attachment. Residents pay attention to the health of downtown because it is their most convenient shopping district and often their place of work.

They care about the city school system because their children live within its boundaries (and because Portland does not have a strong tradition of elite private schooling). Involvement in city politics protects their neighborhoods as well as their business investments. In simplest terms, they "claim" Portland because they can see the heart of the city from living room windows, verandas, and back decks.

The West Hills blend easily into a set of high status suburbs close to the central city. Because Portland's Urban Growth Boundary (see Chapter 3) makes it difficult to create low density, high cost martini farms for a semi-landed gentry, the metro area has no equivalent of the Connecticut or Bucks County, Pennsylvania exurbs. Instead, it boasts very nice houses on moderately sized lots. Dunthorpe, Lake Oswego, Tualatin, and West Linn extend the pleasant and relatively liberal neighborhoods of west side Portland beyond the city limits. A good comparison is the way that Bethesda and Chevy Chase extend affluent northwest Washington beyond the District of Columbia.

Two or three ticks to the political left are socially concerned activists (like me and Barbara Roberts) who earn their incomes in transactional and professional services. Old neighborhoods of business proprietors are now filled with new professional populations. On the west side these folks leaven the social and political mix of high status neighborhoods, helping elect Democratic legislators in what might superficially look like safe Republican territory.[12] On the east side are upper middle class neighborhoods such as Eastmoreland, Laurelhurst, Irvington, Alameda, and Grant Park and mid-status neighborhoods such as Overlook, Ladd's Addition, Sellwood, University Park, and Piedmont (promoted a century ago as "The Emerald, Portland's Evergreen Suburb, Devoted Exclusively to Dwellings—A Place of Homes").

All these neighborhoods date to the first quarter of the twentieth century, when bridges and trolleys made the east side a serious option for middle class Portlanders who wanted to put distance

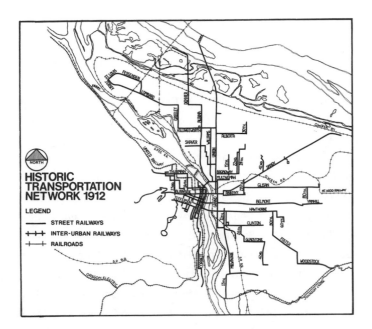

**HISTORIC
TRANSPORTATION
NETWORK 1912**

LEGEND

——— STREET RAILWAYS
+++ INTER-URBAN RAILWAYS
+—+ RAILROADS

Streetcar routes in 1912 (City of Portland). By 1912 streetcar lines served most of the east side to a distance of six miles from downtown. The trolleys supported the growth of a fine-grained mix of working class and middle class neighborhoods.

between themselves and the raucous waterfront. Early twentieth-century real estate developers understood how strongly their clients desired to maintain social distinctions, using restrictive deed covenants to maintain social and ethnic uniformity. Promoters for the Northeast Portland neighborhood of Alameda were typical:

**View, Air, Sunshine, A Fitting Homesite—A Golden Investment is what is offered you at ALAMEDA PARK. The place for the home is coming to be recognized as of more real importance than costly architecture. The best districts of the most progressive cities no longer "just grow up" but are rather selected for their beauty of topography, their convenience to transportation, and are then laid out by the landscape gardener to conserve the natural beauty. . . .**

**. . . the property was laid out by the well known landscape gardener, Mr. Olm-**

CHAPTER 2

sted . . . and was first placed on sale early in the year 1908. . . . At this writing, October 15, 1910, the water mains are laid throughout the older and major portion; cement walks and curbs are rapidly nearing completion; the gas mains are being installed; arrangements to commence the sewer system are now being perfected. Hard surface paving will start upon completion of the pipe laying, and cluster street lamps and ornamental shade trees will follow in order. . . .

Upon completion of the Broadway Bridge [1913], Alameda Park will be even more accessible from the West Side. . . . There will then, in effect, be no river. The fact that the Broadway car line, for its entire course, runs through a restricted residence district insures a desirable class of fellow passengers.

In the greater portion of the Park the building restriction is $500. However, the choicer lots carry a building restriction of $3500. All homes must be built twenty feet back from the property lines. No business houses are allowed except on certain lots at the extreme corner of the tract. Apartment houses, flats, hotels, and stables are taboo—likewise people of undesirable colors and kinds.[13]

The east side boomed. Its population passed that on the west side in 1906 and was double that of the west side by 1916. Reform-minded east side voters in 1913 provided the narrow margin to convert Portland from a somewhat corrupt mayor-council system to the new, progressive commission system of governance with at-large elections. In Portland as elsewhere, the shift undermined indigenous democratic socialism and put government firmly in the hand of the middle class. The last two generations of automobile-based growth have added medium priced over-the-hill neighborhoods on the west side such as Hillsdale and Burlingame.

Residents of these districts are easy to caricature as quality-of-life liberals. During recent years of affluence it has been simple to highlight contradictions—BMWs and Birkenstocks in the same household, or Range Rovers sporting special salmon-saver license plates (nineteen extra dollars a year go to state restoration efforts). But inside the doors of the bungalows, period revival houses, and "old Portland" houses with umbrella-like overhanging eaves, there

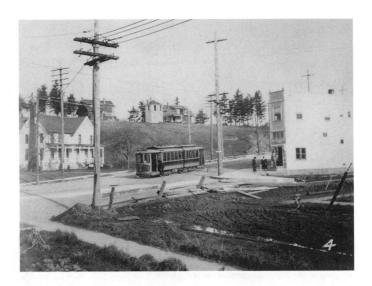

N.E. Sandy and 57th (Oregon Historical Society Neg. 81110). The streetcar city is under construction at Northeast Sandy Boulevard and 57th Street in the 1910s. Speculative commercial space is going up along Sandy, while small builders are beginning to fill in the adjacent blocks a few houses at a time.

is also a culture of civic engagement through neighborhoods, civic organizations, and local government.

At the heart of this civic activism was a "neighborhood revolution" that began when more than a score of neighborhoods began to argue vigorously for their own versions of local revitalization in the later 1960s. By 1971 and 1972, active neighborhood associations and planning committees had established a presence that politicians and planning administrators could not have ignored even had they wanted to do so. Indeed, the critical mass of neighborhood protest required attention not as single problems or single neighborhoods but as a neighborhood movement.

The origins of the movement were different in every section of the city. Portlanders now tend to remember the group with which they were directly involved as the first to storm the barricades of the

City Hall establishment. In fact, the process of neighborhood mobilization began on the east side with local efforts to influence federally assisted programs. Northeast neighborhoods helped to plan and implement a Model Cities program (1966–73) that challenged kneejerk racism and dismayed many bureaucrats. Portland Action Committees Together, a local antipoverty agency, helped organize half a dozen neighborhoods in southeast Portland to participate in community action programs (1967–68). Southeast Uplift (1968) was a locally organized equivalent of Model Cities for the entire set of southeast neighborhoods that had developed in the early twentieth century. A group of southeast neighborhoods in 1972–74 also took the lead in blocking the so-called Mount Hood Freeway, whose five-mile length would have destroyed 1700 houses and apartments and devastated half a dozen neighborhoods.

In the same years, the neighborhood movement gained many of its articulate spokespersons among middle class "colonists" who had begun to recycle (or even gentrify) the older neighborhoods between downtown and the West Hills. The Northwest District Association formed in 1969 to deal with a proposed hospital expansion. It worked with the Planning Bureau from 1970 to 1972 to develop an alternative plan that would preserve Northwest as a high density residential area of Victorian and post-Victorian houses and early twentieth-century apartments. Its mix of students, the elderly, second generation immigrants, and younger professionals makes it Portland's most cosmopolitan neighborhood. The Hill Park Association also organized in 1970 to fight the possible clearance of the Lair Hill neighborhood, located just south of the downtown urban renewal zone; it joined the Corbett, Terwilliger, and Lair Hill neighborhoods to develop their own district plan to preserve fragments of old South Portland and Fulton.

The cooperative effort between the Planning Commission and the Northwest District Association was the catalyst for giving neighborhood groups a formal role in city decisions. City Council established

Mount Hood Freeway (City of Portland). The Mount Hood Freeway, superimposed on this aerial view of Southeast Portland, would have run six miles from I-5 to I-205. Blocked by community action in the early 1970s, it would have obliterated the blocks between Southeast Division and Clinton Streets—blocks that now contain a mix of moderate price housing, community development corporation rehabs, and what even Portlanders view as funky businesses.

the Office of Neighborhood Associations in 1974 to assist local organizations through central and district offices (also see Chapter 3). A quarter century later, neighborhood associations remain important actors on local issues. They are independent bodies that receive city support staff and communication funds. The greatest advantage of formal recognition is a reserved seat at bureau and city council discussions of issues with neighborhood impact, from zoning changes to liquor license renewals. Formal recognition of neighborhood associations has also opened doors at City Hall for other citizen groups.

Civic democracy overall makes a difference. Portland ranks high in comparison with other cities in the average level of citizen involvement, particularly in "strong participation" activities such as service on committees or direct contact with local government. Jeffrey Berry, Kent Portney, and Ken Thomson in *The Rebirth of Urban Democracy* (1993) note Portland's abundance of channels for citizen participation through advisory committees of all sorts, neighborhood associations, neighborhood planning efforts, and direct contact with city officials. Studying a set of issues around drugs, crime, and homelessness in 1988–92, they found that Portland officials generally make decisions in line with popular preferences. Grassroots participation increases political knowledge and enhances a sense that government is, or can be, responsive. Ideally it offers a middle ground between bureaucratic manipulation and grassroots confrontation.[14]

The same tradition of *neighborhood* planning has caused trouble for Planning Bureau efforts to do multi-neighborhood "community" plans. The Planning Bureau not only notifies neighborhood associations of zoning change requests, but in the 1970s and 1980s it also worked with individual communities on district plans and downzoning proposals to protect residential environments. In the 1990s, however, budget constraints pushed the city toward fewer and more comprehensive plans for large quadrants of the city. Both working class outer Southeast and middle class Southwest rebelled against the expectation that they should trade off specific neighborhood goals for citywide interests, forcing changes in plans for infill housing and redevelopment.

In turn, the difficulties of district planning are part of a larger resistance to increasing densities in established neighborhoods. Under the regional 2040 plan (see Chapter 3), the city of Portland has agreed to accommodate tens of thousands of new households over the next generation. Compact growth sounds fine in the abstract. It can quickly become an unwanted intrusion when it appears on the ground. Increasingly (although not universally), neighborhoods complain about new apartments, row houses, and accessory apartments: they already have their share of rentals . . . they'll lose their special character . . . traffic is already overwhelming local streets . . . those vacant parcels are really environmentally sensitive open space.

Neighborhood livability has been central for drawing many activists into civic life, but there are broader causes for nearly everyone. There are tree huggers and salmon savers, defenders of gay rights and urban wildlife, arts advocates, peace workers, public transit buffs, advocates for street youth and the homeless, advocates for HIV-AIDS education and for women's health. In the 1997 election, environmentalists proposed and lost a ballot measure that would have restricted grazing along streams to protect fish spawning grounds. Lawn signs and bumper stickers that appeared throughout progressive Portland captured the convergence of environmental values and social progressivism in the slogan "Safe Sex for Salmon."

As the previous paragraph suggests, progressive Portland includes politically active gay and lesbian residents. Inner southeast neighborhoods have long had a concentration of women's bookstores and art galleries, feminist organizations, and lesbian-friendly bars and restaurants. Growing trendiness along streets such as Southeast Hawthorne has recently displaced portions of the lesbian community to racially mixed sections of Northeast such as Alberta Street. The result is the presence of lesbians as a low visibility component of both affordable and middle range neighborhoods.

Portland's progressive reputation has attracted a disproportionate number of former Peace Corps volunteers. "There was room for the idealist here," Charles Lewis told a reporter. "It's possible to be active, get good public policy, and see the results in people's lives." The attractions are political openness, the presence of "like-minded folks," and opportunities for grassroots organizing around environ-mental and community issues.[15]

The economic and social issues of progressive households and neighborhoods overlap with lifestyle issues of the "Gen X" genera-tion. Interwoven among the older Portland neighborhoods is what we might call—to be trendy—www.alt.city. Portland has a reputa-tion for cool, visible among the thriving clubs and bars in the north-ern edge of downtown or any evening along Southeast Hawthorne Boulevard. Barbara Roberts comments that she felt almost too old to live in the Hawthorne district. In contrast, thirty-something Ann Powers, a pop music writer for the *New York Times* and author of *Weird Like Us: My Bohemian America*, commented recently that "I'd live in this neighborhood. Look at these people. They're my tribe. I could be wearing those red leather pants and white sunglasses." [16]

After losing its young people in the long recession of the 1980s, Portland in the last decade of the century became a hot town for people aged 18–35. With Seattle a bit too spendy and pretentious, Portland has become a sort of poor person's Bay Area, with a funky arts scene, coffee houses, and microbreweries. *Slacker* director Richard Linklater in 1991 called it a great city for his movie's name-sakes. A decade later, Ann Powers named it "one of the major out-posts" of the new Bohemia and noted that "it's majorly hot . . . lots of people in New York are talking about Portland." Along with places such as Austin and Boulder, it is on the circuit of tolerant towns that attract recent college graduates. Commented one young person in 1999, "All my friends in Phoenix are saying that they want to move to Portland too. I know that there are a lot of people who are kind of young and hip and want to live here." [17]

The combination of hipness and natural beauty attracts both pro-fessionals and artists. Law firms find it easy to hire some of the sharpest new graduates. There is a strong alternative arts scene around music clubs and performers, writers, animators, and comic book artists. Mark West, the displaced New York poet in Blake Nelson's *Exile* (1997), finds it hard to score heroin in Portland but meets a familiar environment in the bar and club scene.[18] Jon Raymond of *Plazm* magazine commented recently that Portland is accepting of artists, if not necessarily challenging. Much of the edgier arts scene—experimental architecture and public art, alternative theater and performance art—is the product of newcomers who have consciously chosen to work in Portland. They find, perhaps, marginal financial support, but also a cultural and creative environment that takes intellectual life seriously but is supportive rather than cutthroat and has not locked in "right" and "wrong" styles.[19]

Many who aren't attorneys survive economically in what researcher Chris Ertel calls the barista economy, named for the young people who survive by whipping up cappuccinos and lattes in coffee bars.[20] Per capita income in Portland lagged the nation in the 1980s because of statewide recession tied to the wood products industry. Recovery in the 1990s was led by manufacturing, construction, and professional jobs whose good pay levels buoy progressive Portland. But growth has also increased the number of low paid service workers—the bartenders, waiters, and cappuccino kids who help make Portland pleasant and sophisticated. In short, prosperity has created lots of jobs for people who hang out between college and career and those who want to try career alternatives.

The city of the young is united by no single interest. It draws on small Reed College, but less on the self-contained University of Portland, or on Portland State University, with its commuter students and returning adults. There are environmental activists, ecological absolutists, and environmental artists who use writing and the visual arts to undercut the premises of the corporate economy. There are bicycle commuters and bikers with an attitude. *Bicycling* magazine in March 1999 named Portland the best U.S. city for pedalers, and thousands of bike riders enter downtown on the nicest days. An earlier era of hippiness survives in the frequent sighting of outlandishly painted and decorated cars and vans—several sculpture cars, the literary quotes car, abstract expressionist cars. The city's retro aspects were immediately apparent to the publisher of highly hip *Monk* magazine, who reported on the "aging hippy/feminist/slacker" presence in coffee houses and music clubs. The manager of a Southeast Portland nightclub nicely summed up alternative Portland in describing her clientele: "When we first started, we were getting the granola-crunching, bohemian, gay, lesbian, bike-riding local crowd."[21]

A nice conjunction of Birkenstocks and Doc Martins came together a few blocks down the street from Barbara Roberts. Architect Mark Lakeman in 1995 helped some residents of the Sellwood neighborhood build an impromptu "T-Hows" on a vacant lot. The piece of guerrilla architecture in "woodsy-recycled" style served for a year as a community meeting place. Share-it Square (at Southeast Sherrett Street and Ninth Avenue) followed—an ad hoc piazza painted on the intersection with streetside places to leave produce and household goods for exchange. Some residents loved it and some hated it, but everyone in the neighborhood had an opinion about civic space. In January 2000 City Council adopted an "Intersection Repair Ordinance," allowing intersection developments that promote community interaction if 80 percent of residents within two blocks agree.

Lakeman's City Repair project has followed with mobile teahouses that travel the Portland parks as temporary gathering places. Continuing the clever names, the T-Horse aims at the general public. Teen-Pony, a customized pickup with extendable twenty-foot tent wings, is intended as a gathering place for homeless and marginal teens. The goal of City Repair is "to return the important places of communication and participation to our neighborhoods."[22] Lakeman sees his work as the spiritual successor of the civic activism that created Waterfront Park in the 1970s and Pioneer Courthouse Square in the 1980s—projects to which his father, architect Richard Lakeman, contributed. The purpose is to make spaces for civic life:

for assembly, celebration, politics. The underlying assumption is the quintessential progressive valuation of civic conversation—the belief that more talk among more people will always help.

## ALBINA COMMUNITY DEVELOPMENT

In the bad old days of the 1950s and 1960s, the city desk of *The Oregonian* had what it called "Albina stories." Reports of crime or disorder in a large swath of north and northeast Portland were identified as occurring in Albina. Originally the name of an independent industrial suburb that consolidated with Portland in 1891, "Albina" by the 1940s had become shorthand for the neighborhoods into which the real estate market was pushing African Americans. Although voting patterns and political preferences sometimes make Albina look like a part of Progressive Portland, the importance of race as an American dividing line defines it as a distinct social ecology.

For a window into the district, we can look at Columbia Villa, a neighborhood the city fathers never wanted to build. Portlanders had responded to the Federal Housing Act of 1937, which authorized the creation of local housing authorities to build low rent public housing, by voting nearly 2 to 1 in 1938 against establishing a housing authority. "Unadulterated communism entirely" is what one City Council member called public housing.[23]

The expansion of defense contracts and the attack on Pearl Harbor changed affordable public housing from communism to patriotic duty. City Council chartered the Housing Authority of Portland on December 11, 1941. The Housing Authority broke ground for Columbia Villa in north Portland early in 1942. Like many housing projects of the same era, its 478 units were grouped in one-story duplexes and fourplexes on curving streets with generous lawns that gave it the garden apartment look. For its first twenty years, Columbia Villa housed war workers, returning veterans, and working class families

Albina in 1905 (Oregon Historical Society Neg. 54268). Modest homes and church steeples characterized the immigrant neighborhoods of North Portland. This view from 1905 shows the corner of Russell and Williams Streets in the present-day Eliot neighborhood.

getting their start. Gladys McCoy, the first African American to serve on the Multnomah County Commission, remembered that "Our marriage started in Columbia Villa. . . . We were all married, all with families. . . . We were poor but aspiring." [24]

Columbia Villa and the adjacent Tamarack Apartments (built in 1967) began to slip in the 1970s with changed rules for choosing public housing tenants, persisting poverty, and the spread of heroin addiction. *Night Dogs*, Kent Anderson's novel of police work in 1970s Portland, opens with "the kid who'd OD'd in a gas station bathroom. . . . The needle was still in his arm, half-full of the China White heroin that was pouring in from Southeast Asia, through Vancouver, B.C., and down the freeway." [25] The Villa hit bottom in the 1980s. Many of its single parent households were chronically poor. Crack cocaine and gangs made the streets and lawns unsafe. Columbia Villa didn't look like Cabrini-Green, but it faced many of the same problems as a dead-end environment for dead-end lives.

Recovery began in 1988. A group of civic leaders, including Gladys McCoy, decided to turn Columbia Villa-Tamarack into a miniature Model Cities project. The county sheriff's department began

"Bicycle Kids at Columbia Villa," 1995 (Barry Peril). Barry Peril made a series of photographs of Columbia Villa residents for an exhibit sponsored by the Oregon Council for the Humanities. These "Bicycle Kids" show the neighborhood's "suburban" character. The Villa's many ethnic groups mix more easily as children than as adults.

intensive patrols and community policing with an office on site. The Health Department and Headstart offered onsite programs. The Housing Authority and school district assigned social workers, who helped to develop a Residents' Council to take on maintenance responsibilities and a foot patrol. By 1993–94, when I became acquainted with the new Columbia Villa through an Oregon Council for the Humanities project, reputation and reality had both changed. "The residents have decided they're not going to put up with it [crime]," said one resident in 1994. Now "it's a pleasure to invite my kids and grandkids over for a picnic." After all, she added, "we're not dumb, only poor." [26]

Columbia Villa introduces several themes for understanding the past and future of minorities and the poor. First, Portland poverty is multiethnic. The Villa's population is about 40 percent black, 40 percent native white, 10 percent Hispanic, and 10 percent Russian and Ukrainian immigrant. The larger Albina is similarly home to blacks, Latinos, Native Americans, recent immigrants, and whites. Second, the scale of social and economic disadvantage in Portland is manageable. Third, the manageable scale means that community-based approaches to crime prevention and economic improvement can work, as they have in Columbia Villa.

The small size of the black population is a distinct advantage for maintaining progressive Portland. Because demographic change has been slow, few neighborhoods were challenged by the massive racial change that fueled a generation of racial conflict in Chicago or Detroit. Even in the 1990s, black faces were not common outside downtown and northeast neighborhoods. Poverty is a problem for black Portlanders, but Portland poverty is largely white.

It is an unhappy American reality that citywide and regional consensus is easier when it is essentially within a single race than when it tries to span racial differences. Most Portland neighborhoods can deal with City Hall, and Portland suburbs with the central city, without worrying that they are opening themselves to racial change.

White Portlanders have still chosen suburban housing for a wide variety of reasons, but racial flight has not been prominent among them. Whiteness and regionalism are convenient allies.

The downside of small numbers is white racism that is sometimes unconscious because unchallenged. Many white residents in outlying parts of the metro area can go for years without encountering African Americans as individuals, a situation unheard of in Atlanta or Washington, D.C. Such white isolation supports a reflexive racism based on national media and newspaper crime reporting rather than personal experience. Even a socially liberal leader such as mayor Bud Clark (1985–92) got into trouble with an offhand remark that he might better understand black problems if he got a suntan—a comment that a politician in New York or Baltimore would have intuitively censored.

Just as Portland's leaders sited Columbia Villa far from the upscale neighborhoods of the city, immigrant and ethnic minorities since the late nineteenth century have had to fit themselves into spaces left by mini-Brahmins and progressive middle class. The result has been a set of stopover neighborhoods that have housed European immigrants (1880–1940), African Americans (1930– ), and more recent immigrants from Asia and Latin America.

In the early years of the twentieth century, the crescent of lower land around the central business district together with inner northeast side neighborhoods housed the overwhelming majority of Portland's racial minorities and its foreign-born. These were Portland's closest equivalent to the large ethnic communities of eastern cities. No single European ethnic group provided the majority of residents in any one neighborhood at the start of the century, but Germans set the tone for Goose Hollow, Irish and then Slavic immigrants for Slabtown in Northwest Portland, Scandinavians for the inner Northwest, Finns and Poles for North Portland, German-Russians for the Sabin district in the Northeast, and Italians for Brooklyn near the Southern Pacific rail yards.

One of the best remembered immigrant neighborhoods is South Portland, a fraction of which survived urban renewal and freeway building as the small Lair Hill Historic District just southeast of the Portland State University campus. From the 1890s to the 1940s, the area between the River and the South Park Blocks and southward from Clay Street was an immigrant community. Its two anchors were Failing School and Shattuck School, the gateways for success in the new world. The housing was a mixture of apartments and small "workingmen's cottages." Italian-Americans clustered particularly in the blocks near the river, where a visitor could find the Sons of Italy and the Christoforo Columbo Society, St. Michael's Church and Italian language movies. Jewish immigrants from Poland and Russia were especially concentrated a few blocks upslope between Fourth and Broadway and served by the social settlement workers at Neighborhood House.

World War II and its shipyard jobs changed ethnic dynamics with a sudden increase of Portland's African American population from 2,000 to 15,000. The weekly *People's Observer* chronicled racial incidents on city buses, harassment by police, conflict with segregated unions, and plans for a segregated USO. Housing lay at the heart of racial tensions. White shipyard workers complained about sharing dormitories with blacks. Neighborhood groups raised loud protests at every rumor of new black residents in their areas. Former City Commissioner J. E. Bennett suggested that Kaiser stop hiring black workers. Mayor Earl Riley agreed in private that the migration threatened Portland's "regular way of life." [27]

The real estate industry had already set the community framework for racial relations. Before World War I, most of Portland's 1000 blacks lived on the downtown fringe north of Burnside, with easy access to hotel and railroad jobs. In the 1930s, Realty Board training materials for new salespeople explicitly defined Albina as the appropriate neighborhood for African Americans. Brokers could lose their licenses if they violated the canon of racial segregation by selling houses in all white neighborhoods to minorities. By 1940 more than half of Portland's 2000 African-Americans lived in Albina, with others scattered through other old neighborhoods. Over the next generation, the center of the black community moved more than a mile north, from Williams Avenue and Broadway in 1940 to Martin Luther King, Jr. Boulevard and Skidmore Street by the 1980s, replacing immigrants from the Baltic nations (Sweden, Denmark, Finland, Poland). The process started with land clearance for the Coliseum in the 1950s and continued with the construction of I-5 in the 1960s and the Emanuel Hospital redevelopment in the 1970s in the historic heart of Albina.

We can trace the location and turnover of Portland's ethnic neighborhoods from the public buildings and churches that have survived the weight of time. St. Patrick's Church in Northwest Portland dates from 1891, serving working class Irish at the turn of the century, Croatians in the 1920s and 1930s, and now Spanish-speaking Portlanders. Near the old Finnish community hall is St. Stanislaus Church with its congregation of Polish Catholics. Many Northeast Portland churches passed from one ethnic group to its successor. The Free Evangelical Brethren German Church (1904) gained an onion dome and became St. Nicholas Russian-Greek Orthodox in 1930, and then passed to an African-American congregation. The Norsk-Dansk Methodist Episcopal Kirke is now used by an A.M.E. Zion church, with a new cornerstone next to the old.

Portland has no ghetto that approaches the nearly total racial isolation of South Side Chicago or Bedford-Stuyvesant in New York. The degree of racial concentration in the core community has changed little since 1970. According to the most recent data, from the 1996 American Community Survey, the most segregated census tracts were 69 percent and 70 percent African American; four others were more than 50 percent African-American. These tracts with an African American majority all lie along Northeast King. Taken together, their 10,250 African Americans are only one fourth of all African Americans in the metropolitan area. In short, nearly three-fourths of African Americans in the Portland area are a minority within their own neighborhoods as well as within the metro area as a whole.

Only in the last twenty years has the suburban housing market opened to African American families. A gradual suburbanization that was evident in the 1970s continued at its slow pace in the 1980s. The number of new black residents in Clackamas County in the 1980s — approximately 400 — was the same as the number for the previous decade. The same was true for Washington County, where the increments were 900 for the 1970s and 1000 for the 1980s. Data on housing values and home ownership indicate that these suburban African Americans are part of a successful middle class with the same social status as their white neighbors.

Despite these signs of economic success, the 1980s were bad years for the African American community in North-Northeast Portland. Statewide recession meant high unemployment. Tacit redlining by major banks led to disinvestment and roughly 2000 boarded up houses, a small total compared to massive abandonment in Detroit or North Philadelphia, but large for Portland. A hostile police force deepened the rift between blacks and whites. In 1981 two officers tossed four dead possums in front of a black-owned business; many white Portlanders had a hard time understanding why the "prank" outraged African Americans. In 1985, after community uproar over the death of a black detainee subdued with a sleeper hold, some officers sported T-shirts that read "Don't choke 'em, smoke 'em."

As all over the United States, crack cocaine undermined community stability. The crisis of Columbia Villa was repeated in other neighborhoods. Bloods and Crips arrived from California, exploiting and controlling the market for illegal drugs with crack houses and drive-by homicides. The first gang style drive-by shooting shocked the community in 1987, upsetting the careful fiction that it wasn't going to happen here.

At the same time that white Portlanders feared the dangers of black neighborhoods, blacks steered clear of much of Southeast Portland because of neo-Nazis and skinheads, who in November 1988 kicked the life out of Ethiopian immigrant Mulugeta Seraw. Writing for *The Nation*, journalist Elinor Langer noted the "acute degree of painfully personal racial discomfort" on both sides of the racial divide. To young skinheads, sharing a city with black gangs and assertive black youth *was* dangerous because it *felt* dangerous. "Portland has, in the lifetime of this generation, changed from an informally segregated city to an open one," Langer wrote in 1990, "and the resulting encounters between young people of different races at times and places adults rarely tread have left a wake of ill feeling that the city's predominantly liberal political establishment has been slow to acknowledge." [28]

The crisis of the 1980s triggered a retooling of law enforcement. With Columbia Villa as a positive test, the Portland City Council and police bureau embraced community policing. Police chiefs Tom Potter (1990–93) and Charles Moose (1993–99) worked hard to spread a philosophy of community partnership through the ranks. Relations between police and community became far better than in the 1980s. Police officers work with neighborhood associations and community policing is now coordinated with community-based prosecutors who have flexibility in crafting enforcement strategies over problems such as drug houses.

Statistical analysis and comparisons with other cities offer positive and negative evaluations of black Portland. The level of black-white segregation in the metropolitan area was close to national averages. Data compiled by urban analyst David Rusk show that just over half of poor blacks lived in census tracts with moderately high poverty (those with 20 percent of all residents living in poverty); a figure of three-quarters is more common. Only a quarter of Portland's black poor lived in high poverty tracts (those with 40 percent or more of all residents in poverty). Portland has a troubled ghetto core of intense black poverty, but it is not a *large* district. Black family structure is also more stable than in many large cities, with 93 married black couples with children in 1990 for every 100 black single mothers (in very few metropolitan areas is the number of couples higher than the number of single mothers). The profile on both points was similar to that of the white collar cities of Tallahassee and Charlotte.[29]

Community cooperation in crime control has combined with a booming regional housing market to attract white reinvestment in previously ignored and impoverished neighborhoods. Again because of the racially mixed character of such neighborhoods, gentrification is viewed as much in class as in racial terms. The black middle class has benefited from a booming economy that has translated high levels of homeownership into wealth. The wider public is rediscovering parts of the city that the majority had written off in the 1970s and 1980s. On Northeast Alberta Street, reinvestors include professional basketball star Terrell Brandon (a Portland native but not a Portland player), two community development corporations, and a growing contingent of white artists and gallery owners looking for affordable space. Martin Luther King, Jr. Boulevard, a prime strip for prostitutes in the 1980s, is the site for symbolically important investments by professional sports businesses: Adidas, Nike, and Trail Blazers.

If the 1990s brought more positive public policies, the reason was not traditional political clout. With small numbers, black Portlanders have no prospect of gaining control of the city by voting themselves into power; there is no Richard Hatcher, Coleman Young, or Maynard Jackson in the city's future. Instead, Portland struggles to live up to its progressive ethos as a meritocracy. The professions reward individual competence, especially in government and education. An

African American mayor is a reasonable possibility for the future, but voters will be swayed much more by managerial credentials than by race. African Americans in 1999 conducted the Oregon Symphony, presided over Portland State University, and headed the city school system, parks department, and police department. Blacks are well represented on public committees. A City Club analysis of forty Portland or Multnomah County advisory boards and decision making committees in 1992 found that 12 percent of the members were African Americans, twice the percentage in the total county population. With such a small population base, of course, it is often hard to tell proportional representation from tokenism.

Small numbers mean that Portland's African Americans have to pursue public goals in a political system dominated by whites. The choice has been to revisit the terms of Gunnar Myrdal's classic *The American Dilemma* and appeal to the fundamental values of the American Creed by stressing entrepreneurship and education. Debates over school integration have thus revolved around educational quality and outcomes rather than questions of community control. The central city avoided systematic court-ordered busing in the 1970s by eliminating middle grades in many black neighborhood schools, dispersing black students among a number of middle schools in largely white areas. The school board used magnet programs in the arts, business, and languages to encourage integration of high schools. Protests led by the activist Ron Herndon and the Black United Front in 1980 and 1981 (one-day boycotts by black students, disruption of school board meetings) secured a new middle school in Albina and—more important—focused debate on equalization of student performance.

The issue of achievement has remained at the center of black community politics. Although elementary schools have become slightly more segregated since the 1980s, demands have continued to center on the school system's accountability for improved results—easily measured now that Oregon school policy emphasizes benchmark tests to assess student achievement. African Americans in the Portland schools typically trail white students by a year or more in math and reading, while Latinos lag two years. The data recently brought Herndon out of "retirement" (that is, a career as director of Albina Head Start and president of the National Head Start Association). The Crisis Team of activists and parents in 1999 and 2000 identified a list of underachieving schools needing immediate improvement and organized a new round of protests at school board meetings. The goal remains that of the liberal revolutions of the eighteenth and nineteenth centuries: equal opportunity to pursue lives and careers commensurate with individual talents.

## SILICON SUBURBS

In June 1998 James Howard Kunstler, the acerbic author of *The Geography of Nowhere*, joined Gresham Mayor Gussie McRobert on a ride-along through Portland's largest suburb. If the goal was to strike some sparks for the accompanying reporters, the morning bus ride was a success. McRobert described a community planning and visioning process in which residents of the large east side city expressed a clear preference for efficient development and a real city center. She pointed out apartments along the light rail line and a vital downtown with new shops, library, and city offices. Kunstler acknowledged Gresham's progress from nowhere to someplace during the 1990s, but also fired back by citing "automobile slums" and strip developments no different from any American suburb. "He listened patiently," reported *The Oregonian*, "as McRobert described Gresham's tiny "high tech" corridor of LSI Logic and Fujitsu, but when he commented it was to talk about the superiority of European parks."[30]

McRobert was certainly correct. A classic Portland progressive, she has worked for compact and civil communities as mayor, as member of state commissions, and chair of the "smart growth" organization Livable Oregon. She has helped to lead her community and region in the direction of compact development envisioned by regional plans. The October 1999 groundbreaking for Gresham's "Civic Neighborhood" was a vindication for her vision. Originally slated for a regional mall, the eighty acres have been replatted with a street grid and rezoned for a mix of housing, offices, and street-oriented shops. Adjacent to Gresham's downtown and served by the area's first light rail line, the district will help to anchor Gresham as the regional center for eastern Multnomah County.

But Kunstler was also correct. Even acknowledging the work of McRobert and other regional leaders ("Gresham is doing better than just about any city in America"), he noted the generic suburban landscapes he has attacked in his books ("But they need to do better").[31] Gresham has new supermarkets in berry fields, shopping center strips, and an automobile dealer corridor that starts just where light rail stops. Many parts of Clark, Clackamas, and Washington Counties look the same. An occasional big box bookstore with a latte bar does not counteract the impact of three superregional malls.

Much of "silicon suburbia," in short, is indistinguishable from the generic U.S. suburb. Portland suburbs have plenty of people (65 percent of the PMSA), plenty of jobs (45 percent of the PMSA), and large stretches of standard postwar cityscapes. Workers leave standard model subdivisions and apartment tracts to battle clogged suburban highways in order to reach jobs in commercial strips and office parks. Big box retail stores compete with precast concrete manufacturing boxes and landscaped corporate headquarters for prime acreage. Mile by mile, much of Washington and Clackamas Counties looks like the suburbs of Denver or Dayton, with garden apartments, 1960s-era split level houses, strip malls, and the pseudo chateaux of the '90s.

I've termed these areas silicon suburbs because the electronics industry has driven their recent growth in the counties and communities that ring Portland. The so-called "Silicon Forest" is the combined result of entrepreneurial accident and location. The core of the industry from the 1950s to the 1970s was Tektronix, a homegrown manufacturer of oscilloscopes and other measuring devices, along with several spinoff companies. One close observer of the industry comments that Tek "had the best experts in the field. It might as well have been a university—it was a great finishing school for entrepreneurs."[32]

The scene changed in 1976 when Intel chose Portland for a major branch plant. One attraction was the pool of workers trained by Tek, the other was a location only two hours from San Jose. Hewlett-Packard followed in 1979, Wacker Siltronics in 1980, and two waves of Japanese firms in the later 1980s and 1990s—SEH, Sharp, Fujitsu, Epson, NEC—attracted in part by the city's closeness to Tokyo by the great circle air route. Although not all the facilities will be built, outside electronics firms in 1996–97 announced plans for investment of $10 billion in metropolitan Portland. The region's specializations are semiconductors and display technologies. The 47,000 manufacturing and 14,000 software jobs (as of 1997) are thickest on the west side of the metropolis where chip plants and software firms form an arc from Hillsboro to Wilsonville, clinging to U.S. 26, Oregon 17, and I-5. Clark County, with 5000 workers in two large plants, comes next, followed by Gresham and then by Portland, with one large wafer plant and a cluster of downtown software writers.[33]

The tilt toward the western suburbs has run counter to the older eastward expansion that began with the streetcar suburbs of the early twentieth century. Immediately after World War II, the prime target for suburban growth was eastern Portland and Multnomah County, served by the area's first freeway, which crept slowly into the city from Troutdale. Builders followed the wedge of high, buildable land that pointed toward Gresham between the Columbia River flood plain and Johnson Creek. Eastern Multnomah County beyond the city limits added 80,000 residents during the 1940s and 1950s.

These new communities matched the popular image of the bedroom suburb. They sent 64 percent of their workers on the daily commute to the city of Portland in 1960 and 55 percent in 1970. The proportion of residents who had moved into eastern Multnomah County directly from the central city was twice that for the other metropolitan area counties. The signs that marked the city limits of Portland in the early 1960s defined a political but not a social boundary.

Highway building shifted the subdivision frontier from east side to west side. The Sunset Highway (U.S. 26) in 1960 and I-5 in 1963 followed a 1944 recommendation by Robert Moses, creating high speed, high capacity auto routes over the West Hills. Route 217 connected the two highways in 1965, just in time to serve high tech industry. Washington and Clackamas Counties began to outpace Multnomah County in the 1960s. Washington County's share of metropolitan population leaped from 11 percent to 19 percent, and Clackamas County's share from 14 percent to 20 percent. The new neighborhoods between Portland and Gresham had been built in the 1940s and 1950s for Americans just rediscovering affluence. Small one-story houses filled neighborhoods that sometimes lacked sidewalks, street lighting, or sanitary sewers. Many of the suburban streets and houses of Washington County were built during the high tide of prosperity in the 1960s and early 1970s. The average Washington County house in 1970 was bigger, newer, and better equipped than its counterpart in Multnomah County—and 30 percent more expensive. The 1970s, 1980s, and 1990s reinforced the predominance of the west side for new housing and office development. Population data show that Washington County outpaced all its metropolitan neighbors until the 1990s, when Clark County surged into first place (Table 3).

Furthering the process of suburban maturation, industrial development in Washington County has created a modern equivalent of nineteenth-century company neighborhoods where workers clustered close to new jobs. Nearly 61 percent of Washington County residents worked within the county in 1990 rather than commuting

TABLE THREE   County Population Growth Rates, 1970–2000 (percent)

| County | 1970–80 | 1980–90 | 1990–2000 |
|---|---|---|---|
| Clackamas | 46 | 15 | 19 |
| Clark | 50 | 24 | 45 |
| Columbia | 24 | 5 | 15 |
| Multnomah | 1 | 4 | 12 |
| Washington | 56 | 27 | 39 |
| Yamhill | 38 | 18 | 28 |

to the central city or to other outlying job centers (for Clackamas County the comparable figure is only 46 percent).

Firms that depend on Japanese and Korean managers and investors have helped enhance the ethnic/immigrant dimension of the industrialized Sunset Corridor. Washington County—particularly in the Beaverton area—houses a modern version of nineteenth-century immigrant communities. Foreign-born technicians and engineers are an important part of the high tech labor force. So are the East Asian immigrants who staff Silicon Forest chip plants. The county's Asian origin population shot from 5000 to 14,000 during the 1980s. Inner Washington County now has important concentrations of Korean, Vietnamese, and other Asian American business and institutions.

Old and new Asian Americans offer a contrast of old and new neighborhoods. Groups with long tenure in Portland maintain community institutions in their old downtown waterfront neighborhoods: the Chinese Consolidated Benevolent Association in a refurbished nineteenth-century building, the Japan-American Society with a history museum in the heart of the old Japantown. The majority of Korean churches, businesses, and organizations are found in Beaverton and environs. A pan-Asian supermarket in Beaverton has supplanted most old ethnic food stores. On a Saturday morning it has a bit of the multinational bustle of Singapore.

In spite of its apparent tendency to reproduce Santa Clara County, California, Washington County has not yet emerged as an "edge city" that has declared its independence of the city of Portland. The central city remains the location for vital business, professional, and medical services. Nor does Washington County contain any key metropolitan public facilities — sports complex, convention center, airport, port, comprehensive university, flagship museum, major recreational attraction. Specialists on the multinodal city can identify only one "edge city" (Joel Garreau's term, applied to Beaverton-Tigard-Tualatin triangle) or "suburban activity center" (Robert Cervero's term, applied to the I-5 corridor from Tigard to Wilsonville).[34] Even these are incomplete examples at best. Instead, the outer ring of the metropolitan area remains closely tied to the core through a radial highway system and a developing radial rail system.

The silicon suburbs are the least "Oregon" part of the metropolitan area. Only four of the ten largest electronics firms are controlled locally. High tech growth now has its own momentum. It drives the needs for workers and public services (Intel in July 2000 announced plans to add 6000 more jobs in the Hillsboro area), and it explains why manufacturing jobs in Portland grew by 2.5 percent a year from 1990 to 1997 while manufacturing jobs in all U.S. metropolitan areas shrank by 0.4 percent annually. The high education levels required for many of the new jobs have widened the gap with the old economy. All in all, the suburban industrial profile overall is closer to Austin, Texas than to traditional Oregon communities.

## METROPOLITAN BORDERLANDS: THE COUNTRY IN THE CITY

One weekday morning in April 1990, hundreds of logging trucks converged on downtown Portland. Usually seen barreling down graveled mountain roads on the metropolitan fringe or growling along freeways on the way to export docks, the trucks were a city surprise. With deep pitched horns blaring and engines rumbling, the big rigs circled the blocks around Pioneer Courthouse Square. Their drivers were angry about limitations on timber harvests from the identification of spotted owls as an endangered species. They took their protest into the stronghold of their perceived enemies, the city based environmentalists whose support of the Endangered Species Act seemed to value birds over working families and their way of life.

When the residents of progressive Portland talk about "the country in the city," they are thinking about the preservation of wetlands, open fields, nesting sites, and wooded wildlife corridors. But the phrase can take on a second meaning that links it to the frustrated loggers. Extensive county boundaries spread the metropolitan area over miles of farms and large tracts of commercial woodlands. They reach far into Mount Hood National Forest and touch the Siuslaw and Gifford Pinchot National Forests. These parts of the old West are the country within the metropolis. The towns and back acres are populated by people who value the natural environment as a source for jobs, as private property, and as a commons for individual use. Some communities retain their traditional identities. Others have been engulfed and transformed by urbanization. All coexist somewhat uneasily with silicon suburbs and progressive city neighborhoods. From the standpoint of the foothills towns, Portland substitutes paperwork for real work. It has long been the exploiter whose bright lights seduced the young, the dangerous place of confusing size and social variety.

These are marginal landscapes in several senses. They are situated on the metropolitan fringe between the suburbs and the uninhabited forests. Old forestry and mill towns are also increasingly marginal to the metropolitan economy. Farm towns are more successful at retaining their original economic functions but are increasingly engulfed and altered by exurban growth that jumps Portland's Urban Growth Boundary and the agricultural greenbelt. These are not necessarily poor communities, but neither do long time residents fully share big city prosperity. Urban analyst Myron Orfield has divided Portland suburbs into those with high and low property values. In most metropolitan areas the low property value suburbs are aging communities adjacent to the aging central city. For Portland, in contrast, they are mostly towns on the farm-forest fringe: Forest Grove, Cornelius, Banks, North Plains, and Gaston in Washington County, Canby, Molalla, Estacada, and Sandy in Clackamas County.[35] Orfield did not extend his analysis north of the Columbia, but Clark County in 1990 had lower education levels, lower per capita income, and a smaller proportion of professional and managerial employment than Washington, Clackamas, or Multnomah County.

In 1994 journalist Susan Orlean, who wrote for the Portland alternative weekly *Willamette Week* in the 1980s, tried to capture the character of Portland's blue collar foothills in a *New Yorker* story about ice skater Tonya Harding, notorious for the effort to cripple rival Nancy Kerrigan. The hardscrabble hills of Clackamas County she depicts are no more than ten miles from the upscale Clackamas County suburbs of Lake Oswego and West Linn, but a vast cultural distance.

Portland is the largest city in Oregon, but it is of very little consequence to people like Tonya and Jeff [Gillooly] and Shawn [Eckardt], who live in and rarely leave Clackamas and east Multnomah Counties. News reports that say Tonya is from Portland have missed the geographical and sociological point. The world that Clackamas County is part of starts somewhere in the great Plains, skips over cities like Portland and Seattle, and then jumps to Alaska—a world where people are plunked down on harsh or austere or overgrown landscapes and might depart from them at any moment, leaving behind only a few houses and some gear. Alaska, desolate and rugged and intractable, feels like an annex of Clackamas County, and Portland seems a million miles away. Alaska, not Portland, is also where many people from Oregon have often gone to get more land, or to make quick money by working for a summer in a fish cannery or on a logging crew. There is a Yukon Tavern in Clackamas County and a Klondike Jewelers, and at the nearby thrift stores you can find old table linens with Alaskan motifs—huskies, oil rigs, Eskimos—and old postcards of Alaskan landscapes and photographs of Juneau cannery crews and of log camps, scribbled with messages to the family back in Clackamas.[36]

The social ecology of the metro borderlands is no more than a century old. Logging did not go big time in the Coast Range and the shoulders of Mount Hood until the early twentieth century, as part of the massive relocation of the American lumber business from the Great Lakes to the Pacific Northwest. Industrial logging dwarfed previous land clearance in the Portland region. In Washington and Columbia counties, large scale cutting followed railroads into the Coast Range and onward to Tillamook Bay. Loggers and logging railroads also penetrated the lower slopes of the Cascades from the Clackamas and Columbia rivers. Towns like Estacada and Vernonia are essentially products of this early twentieth century timber boom. So were vanished settlements like Bridal Veil and Palmer on the flank of Mount Hood.

Lying between the forests and the city were the long established county seats that served mature farming districts (Table 4). Oregon City (Clackamas County) remained the most prominent center between Portland and Salem as late as the 1940s. Hillsboro (Washington County) and McMinnville (Yamhill County) reflected the prosperity of Willamette Valley agriculture (as did comparably sized Newberg). The booming development of St. Helens (Columbia County) was a response to the expansion of the Coast Range timber industry. Across the Columbia, the rapid growth of Vancouver, Camas, and Washougal also responded to the wood products industry.

By the 1950s, farm and forest communities were feeling the pressure of the growing city. In *Ricochet River*, Portland writer Robin

TABLE FOUR   Population of County Seats, Portland Metropolitan Area

| City | 1890 | 1910 | 1930 | 1950 |
|------|------|------|------|------|
| Vancouver | 3,545 | 9,300 | 15,766 | 41,664 |
| Oregon City | 3,062 | 4,287 | 5,761 | 7,682 |
| Hillsboro | n.a. | 2,016 | 3,039 | 25,142 |
| McMinnville | 1,386 | 1,651 | 22,917 | 6,635 |
| St. Helens | 220 | 742 | 3,994 | 4,711 |
| Portland | 46,385 | 207,214 | 301,815 | 373,628 |

n.a.: not reported

Cody reached back to his boyhood to describe the changing isolation of "Calamus" (a stand-in for the town of Estacada, about 20 miles southeast of Portland). "The Cliffs were coming up. The road there cuts close to the bank, and you get pipes echoing through the turns. Trees close to the road. Glimpses of Calamus River on the left. It's the best part of the drive to Portland. . . . [But soon] We'd reached the outskirts of the city. Shopping centers, warehouses, housing developments. Like a great living thing, the city was spreading toward Calamus. Yellow Caterpillars prowled the hills, and the smell of fresh asphalt snaked into the car." On his return to the town, Cody's teenaged protagonist reflected: "In the old days you could go Out West. Link [his grandfather] came out West. Gus Schwartz, before him, came Out West. Old Huckleberry Finn, for example, he could light out for the territory. The trouble is, Calamus *is* the territory. Calamus puts you flat up against it, geographically speaking." [37]

The forest fringe allowed Portland to displace social conflict to the woods. Political conflicts in the city were less capitalists versus workers, as in Chicago or Seattle, than businessmen versus the yeomanry of skilled workers and small business owners. Early Portland was not a good town for radical unions except on the waterfront, where shipbuilders struck in 1917, seamen in 1921, and longshoremen in 1934. From the 1910s into the 1930s, Mayor George Baker did the bidding of the business elite by creating a police "red squad" to run union organizers out of town. Police helped break the 1921 strike and weighed in on the side of business in 1934. With some exaggeration, the Chamber of Commerce in 1928 claimed that "the City has always been free from radical sentiment." [38] Relatively well paid and settled urban factory workers, railroad men, and craftsmen could identify with the petit bourgeoisie (Portland in the early twentieth century had an unusually high rate of homeownership). Their preferred avenues of civic action were electoral populism or home-grown socialism. As in smaller eastern cities such as Dayton and Milwaukee, the Socialist Party was strong through 1912—until middle

St. Helens, Oregon (Oregon Historical Society Neg. 0327 A 042). The Pope and Talbot lumber mill dominates the city of St. Helens in this view from the top of the Columbia County court-house taken before World War II. Thirty miles from the center of Portland, St. Helens is one of a half dozen wood products towns that are now incorporated into the metropolitan region.

Estacada Timber Jamboree Court, August 1949 (Oregon Historical Society Neg. 011762). The Estacada Timber Jamboree evolved from informal contests among woods workers to a money-maker sponsored by the local business community. Declining attendance led to its suspension for the decade of the 1990s.

class Portlanders voted to adopt commission government with elections at large that undermined its neighborhood voting base.

The most heavily exploited laborers in the regional economy were unskilled rural workers on farms, railroads, and forests, but even here the culture of the woods ran on rugged individualism. Oregon loggers and mill workers were more likely to identify with the image of self-sufficient mountain men than to join One Big Union. Washington state was the hotbed of the Industrial Workers of the World with its Timber Workers strike in 1917, its "free speech campaigns" in Spokane and Seattle, its violent confrontations in the Everett and Centralia massacres. Portland was the headquarters of the Loyal Legion of Loggers and Lumbermen, a cross between a company union and a patriotic society organized in 1917 to combat the I.W.W.

The result is the persistence of a strongly individualistic "pioneer" culture. Hugh Chance in David James Duncan's novel *The Brothers K* works in the Camas, Washington paper mill but gets in trouble with his union for doing extra work on the side during a strike; family obligations trump solidarity. We've already met Ken Kesey's Hank Stamper, a character who scorns unionization as much as he scorns the Wakonda Auga River. Poet Gary Snyder writes the voice of Ed McCullough, an old logger hanging onto a marginal job in the woods as a knotbumper, smoothing the logs that snorting tractors skidded to the landing:

Ed McCullough, a logger for thirty-five years
Reduced by the advent of chainsaws
To chopping off knots at the landing:
"I don't have to take this kind of shit,
Another twenty years
    and I'll tell 'em to shove it"
    (He was sixty-five then)
In 1934 they lived in shanties
At Hooverville, Sullivan's Gulch.
When the Portland-bound train came through
The trainmen tossed off coal.

"Thousands of boys shot and beat up
For wanting a good bed, good pay,
    decent food, in the woods—"
No one knew what it meant:
"Soldiers of Discontent."[39]

Metropolitan agriculture is in far better shape than metropolitan logging (Verboort in Washington County still stages a sausage festival and Molalla in Clackamas County has a rodeo, while Estacada is trying to revive its timber carnival after a ten-year hiatus). Clackamas County ranks third among Oregon counties in value of agricultural products. Washington County ranks sixth; its farm income rose 40 percent from 1978 to 1992 despite substantial suburbanization. Two other top ten counties are also in the CMSA.[40] Organized agriculture, through the Farm Bureau, fiercely defends state land use laws that offer protection from leapfrog urban development. Serious farmers can make long term investments. Many of them grow specialized high value products: nursery stock, flower bulbs, hops, grass seed, nuts, berries, vegetables for freezing, pinot noir grapes for a thriving wine industry.

The strength of labor-intensive agriculture explains why much of the Latino population of the metropolitan area lives on its outer edges. Migrant workers have become permanent residents in many farm towns. In a town such as Hillsboro, county officials work at outreach in Spanish; Mexican immigrants and high tech employees compete to influence the directions taken by the old county seat. The quality of farm worker housing is a hot local issue. The farmers' market around the perimeter of Hillsboro's courthouse square on a summer Saturday is not Miami or Los Angeles, but it draws a multiethnic crowd. Members of the Washington County Fair Board caused a minor flap in June 2000 when they noted with concern that Hillsboro Happy Days—the Fourth of July festival—now attracts an overwhelmingly Latino crowd with banda music, churro stands, and Mexican singing stars. The problem, it turns out, is that Anglos quit coming to the traditional celebration in the 1990s, while Mexican Americans offered a large and largely untapped market for festival organizers.

At the same time that the country moves into the suburbs, the city invades the substantially rural counties on the metropolitan fringe — Clark, Columbia, Yamhill—with mixed results. Old families lament the end of small town folksiness as commuters fill new subdivisions. North of the Columbia River, a group of rural residents dissatisfied with creeping suburbanization tried (unsuccessfully) in 1996 to split the farms and small towns of Clark County's northern half into a separate county. Nearly half the workforce of Scappoose in Columbia County, Oregon make the drive into Portland, but to be called a "commuter suburb" deeply violates the town's self-image. "There is a deep-seated fear in people who have lived here of being swallowed by Portland—of being forced to be city dwellers," said former County Commissioner Bruce Hugo in 1998. "People move here because they want to live in a rural environment, but they are kidding themselves saying they can have it both ways." Newcomers place unexpected demands on schools and other services. "We are suffering from an influx of people," complaints Jeff VanNatta, a fifth generation resident of Columbia County. "The newcomers don't work in this county. They work in Portland, they shop in Portland, and they drive home and they complain about the roads." [41]

Most towns, including Scappoose, retain a business core of downtown merchants, realtors, attorneys, and insurance agents. They join the Kiwanis, staff Chamber of Commerce committees, and boost the high school football team. These are "traditionalists" in Adam Davis's typology. Steeped in the values of Main Street, they are the members of miniature growth machines who see the benefits of rising property values and more customers for shops and service businesses. They are the potential supporters of "Main Street" downtown redevelopment efforts and sometimes—in self-contradiction—the backers of Wal-Mart and highway strip development. Along with progressive Portland, these are the places where churches, associations, and other civic institutions are most dense.

Let's visit Yamhill County between Portland and Salem. Blessed with fertile valleys and sunny hillsides, the county's diversified farming has long supported a prosperous set of small towns. In the last twenty years of the twentieth century, however, growth has come fast. The landscape now reveals the economic patterns that caused

Census Bureau analysts to add the county to metropolitan Portland in the 1980s. Motorists clog the major through corridor of Oregon 99W during daily rush hours. Sunday afternoons and evenings can be even worse as Portlanders return home from weekends on the coast. On the edges of towns like Newberg and on the hills over-looking once tiny Dundee are new houses for commuters to Salem offices and Hillsboro electronics plants.

Dundee itself is surprisingly fashionable as the center of Oregon's wine industry. In the last quarter century, Yamhill County has gained 2600 acres of vineyards and forty wineries. Dundee boosters see a tasteful Oregon version of the Napa Valley, especially with the Mondavi and Beringer operations looking to invest. The town has wineries, tasting rooms, and a growing list of fine restaurants. Twenty years ago Dundee was a center of the Oregon hazelnut business. Now, say its boosters, it is in the middle of "an increasingly cosmopolitan valley with a cutting edge." [42] In fact the transition is far from complete. Many of the wineries can be reached by paved roads from 99W, but the way in from the "country" side may well be a rutted gravel road.

Yamhill's county seat, McMinnville, is an old riverboat town that has jumped in a generation from a few thousand to 25,000 residents. Big box retailers and discount stores line the highway from Portland to the coast. Fighting back, the old downtown has replaced general purpose retailing with restaurants and boutiques. Farm and factory workers stock up at K-Mart while day tourists and the middle class enjoy a revived town center. Meanwhile, preparations continue to open an aviation museum with its main attraction the Spruce Goose, Howard Hughes's notorious failed prototype for a supersized cargo plane. It may prove a good draw for the tourist trade, but it is a roadside attraction with little connection to the community's past.

On the opposite side of the metropolitan area, a huge paper mill still looms over downtown Camas, Washington, just as David James Duncan described it for the 1960s:

The night lights have all come on—whole constellations of them—spotlights and floodlights and huge square-bulbed power lights, suspended and shining from walls and wires, lighting the fog from here to the middle of the Columbia. The mill's got . . . wings as big as office buildings, with snarls of exposed vents and flumes and overhead or underground pipes feeding them a steady river's worth of water, some of the pipes and flumes big enough to drive semis through; I can count fourteen lighthouse-sized smokestacks just from where we're sitting, with steam pouring so thick out of nine of them that they look like the source of every cloud in earth. I can feel the fog vibrating from the machinery in the building behind the giant clock.[43]

But most of the town's *new* jobs are in a high tech industrial park, located upwind from the mill. Mill workers can still stop at Shorty's Pool Hall and The Mill tavern, but designer jewelry and top-of-the-line bicycles are available two blocks up the tastefully tree shaded, mall-like main drag. The director of the Camas Downtown Association also draws on the image of the Bay Area, claiming that the town is only a few steps away from becoming "the Palo Alto of the Northwest. That's probably going to get me in trouble, but it's true."[44]

If Scappoose and McMinnville and Camas show some of the ways that the expansion of metropolitan economy and culture affects small towns and their traditional social and economic values, there are a number of low income neighborhoods in which immigrants from the foothills try to recreate rural lifestyles on the edges of the city. Latinos and loggers come together in a number of close-in neighborhoods in Clackamas County and eastern Multnomah County that house country people in the city. Parkrose, Lents, Brentwood-Darlington are refuges and halfway houses for reluctant urbanites. They are areas of mobile home parks, self-built houses, unpaved streets (the property owners can't afford a special assessment district), wealth stored on wheels in old automobiles and trucks and boat trailers and campers, rottweilers behind chain link fences.

At their worst, such "mid-East" blocks have as many problems and dangers as the most troubled sections of North or Northeast Portland. Adam Davis offers the category "alienated strugglers." To a hip outsider looking for the unusual, this is where to find the "weirdest, wackiest, seediest assortment of people and businesses in the Great Northwest."[45] Many residents refuse to open their doors to *any* stranger—political canvasser, salesman, or census taker. Teenagers clump together in Latino and Vietnamese gangs that shake down their compatriots. There are meth labs and pot growers. Vigorous law enforcement downtown and in close-in neighborhoods has pushed prostitution eastward—to cruise strips and hourly motels on 82nd Avenue and Northeast Sandy Boulevard. The Errol Heights neighborhood—since renamed Brentwood-Darlington to get rid of bad overtones—long suffered the cheap-shot nickname "Felony Flats" for the ex-convicts who have ended up in its cheap housing. Inexpensive one- and two-story apartment complexes mix struggling single parent families and drug dealers. In little more than a year, the police compiled a five-inch folder of reports on drug use, beatings, gunfire, and murder in a single 95-unit complex on Southeast 122nd Avenue. The drug-soaked losers in Gus Van Sant's movie *Drugstore Cowboy* are comfortable in the inexpensive houses and motels of such neighborhoods. When one of their group dies of an overdose, they drive up a dirt road into the cutover foothills to dispose of the body. One Multnomah County deputy sheriff commented in 1994 that they kept xeroxed custody sheets on some of the most frequent offenders so they could just fill in the date and time for each arrest.

These same districts are also home to stable working class families. A block of deeply rundown houses can be interrupted with a surprise—a house well kept and newly painted, with well tended lawn and borders of flowers, but still behind its chain link fence. Residents have fierce pride in what they do for themselves. They are willing and able to work together one on one to face down a particularly obnoxious neighbor, but suspicious of much beyond. The district has generated a number of self-help efforts in the last decade (Neighborhood Pride Team, Outer Southeast Caring Community), but its residents are less likely to vote than "progressive Portlanders." Many wish that government would just go away. "There's a definite sense of being the last bastion of rugged individualism," comments the director of the local community center.[46]

Scattered among these marginal neighborhoods are family oriented immigrants whose distrust of government has been well learned. Since 1975 Oregon has ranked eleventh among the states for refugee resettlement. In the 1980s it gained large numbers of Vietnamese, Cambodians, Lao, Hmong, Russians, and Ukrainians. More recent arrivals include Ethiopians, Burmese, Kurds, and Bosnians. About half of Multnomah County's foreign-born live in "Mideast." Several hundred Rumanians have found an economic niche providing adult foster care services through extended families. The CMSA houses an estimated 40,000 to 60,000 Russian-speaking Russians and Ukrainians. Many are self-isolated by evangelistic religion, but the classic trappings of an immigrant community are developing. Several hundred small businesses serve community needs and established immigrants staff many of the agencies that serve even newer arrivals.

Either way, these are people and neighborhoods of stubborn individuals. They don't much trust government and can't imagine getting good value for their tax dollars—the opposite of the progressive core. It was "the government" that ran I-205 through the middle of the Lents business district, and it is "the government" that now arrives with fancy plans for economic revitalization. To the dismay of many residents, Portland and Gresham together annexed nearly 150,000 people in the urbanized portions of eastern Multnomah County between 1984 and 1994, after the county decided to phase out urban services such as police and parks and concentrate on social services.

The result has been tense political battles over the equitable financing of infrastructure for the recently annexed districts. The owners of inexpensive houses on dirt streets find themselves faced with paying their share of paving costs when new houses go in. Suburbs that were semi-rural when first developed in the 1950s and 1960s have filled in as medium density neighborhoods, forcing the replacement of septic systems with costly sewer systems for both health and environmental protection. Many working class homeowners found that annexation was quickly followed with sewer hookup bills of $8,000 to $10,000, causing the Portland Organizing Project in the late 1980s to initiate a long and organizationally exhausting fight with the Portland City Council. The final agreement reduced overall costs and gave individual homeowners a break of at least $2500. And the battle convinced many new Portlanders and Greshamites that their worst fears about downtown politicians and bureaucrats were true.

High school students are sensitive monitors of social boundaries. One of the neighborhoods in transition is Parkrose in eastern Multnomah County. What used to be all white suburbia is now ethnically mixed—one quarter Latino, Asian, and eastern European; what used to be a middle class neighborhood is now poor enough to qualify as a Housing and Community Development target area. Kids know the pecking order of area high schools; theirs is a "food stamp school," says one student.[47] On the other side of the social divide is the silicon suburb of Tigard. A few years ago it joined the "Pac-8" high school football conference, whose other members are larger rural towns in the metropolitan fringe of Portland (Forest Grove, McMinnville, Canby, Newberg) or Salem (Dallas, Silverton). One Tigard player described their reception: "We come in here as the new guys from the city, and here we are going to Dallas and Forest Grove. I feel like we're kind of marked men." [48]

The sophisticated "city" athletes and the food stamp school are the same seven miles from downtown Portland. One represents the outward spread of Portland's core and the understanding that progressive Portland and silicon suburbs have the same sophistication and ride the same wave of prosperity. The other represents fragments of an older society of families pulling together a living from hard work in odd corners of the economy. They are new west and old west, Portland and province, global growth trends worked out in the daily lives of real teenagers.

# The Best Planned City?

## SALMON AND SPIRIT

In 1957 the U.S. Army Corps of Engineers put the finishing touches on The Dalles Dam, the second, counting upstream, of fourteen dams that block the main stem of the Columbia River. The Dalles Dam extended the reach of barge navigation upstream and tapped the stored force of the river for electricity. It is far less massive than Grand Coulee Dam and less important for regional development than Bonneville Dam, but it plays a central role in the narrative of the Pacific Northwest.

A few miles upstream from the dam site, a great basalt dike created Celilo Falls, the beginning of a nine-mile constriction that continued as the Long Narrows (sometimes the Five Mile Rapids) and the Short Narrows. Thrusting out against the current, the basalt's slick black shoulders pinched and funneled the river into surging falls and rapids—"the Dalles" of the French fur traders. Every second, tens of tons of water boiled through the channels and dropped toward the sea. William Clark found Celilo easy to portage but wrote of the Short Narrows that

at this place the water of this great river is compressed into a chanel between two rocks not exceeding *forty five* yards wide and continues for a 1/4 of a mile

Celilo Falls (Oregon Historical Society Neg. 65993). The Dalles Dam drowned Celilo Falls in the late 1950s, ending centuries of fishing by Indian peoples.

when it again widens to about 200 yards and continues this width for about two miles when it is again interspersed by rocks. . . . I determined to pass through this place notwithstanding the horrid appearance of this agitated gut swelling, boiling & whorling in every direction, which from the top of the rock did not appear as bad as when I was in it.[1]

The falls were a challenge for migrating salmon and an opportunity for uncounted generations of native fishermen. The people of the central river built long rickety ramps and platforms over the rocks to overhang the channels. Balanced on slick boards above the spray, they dipped long-handled nets to snag the salmon that leaped upstream. Naturalist David Douglas described the fishing: "Before the water rises on the approach of summer, small channels are made among the stones and rocks . . . over which is placed a platform for a person to stand. . . . [He] then places his net at the top of the channel, which is always made to fit it exactly, and it is carried down with the current. The poor salmon, coming up his smooth and agreeable road as he conceives it to be, thrusts himself into the net and is immediately thrown onto the stage."[2] Women and children clubbed the fish and dragged them to shore to gut, split, and hang on racks to cure in sun and smoke.

As a rich fishery and a barrier to canoes, Celilo and the Long Narrows created a natural trading point. The settled villagers of the lush coast brought fish, shells, cedar wood, cedar bark, baskets, and whalebone. The people of the dry plateaus and mountains brought hides, buffalo robes, pipestone, obsidian, and meat. Visitors haggled, traded, and left to return in following years to this "great emporium or mart of the Columbia, and general theater of gambling and roguery," to quote a critical white trader who visited in 1810.[3] By the early 1800s the people of the lower Columbia had become skilled and active trading partners of the American and British trading companies, adding blankets and other manufactured trade goods to their business.

When the dam closed and the waters rose to drown the surging cascades, Celilo Falls became a dividing point in history as well as space. The death of the falls encapsulated generations of environmental and cultural change in a single event. The alteration of native cultures has been a 200-year process that started with the arrival of British and American trading ships. The destruction of wild salmon stocks has taken 130 years since the advent of industrialized fishing and canning. But the two stories crossed at this single point and time—in the final "first salmon" ceremony in April 1956 and the last season of traditional Celilo fishing. Captured on film and in memory, the last season of fishing is far more vivid than the incremental draining of the Everglades or the gradual alteration of the tall grass prairie. It is not an unfortunate mistake that *they*—our unenlightened ancestors—made out of ignorance. It is something that *we* did—an act whose motivations and consequences remain part of the present.

The conflict of dam building and salmon fishing embodies the modern tension between need for nature's wealth and awareness of natural limits. In retrospect, this is the event that began to change the message of dam making on the Columbia from progress to declension. In the dam-making era, Portlanders and other northwesterners wrote books with titles such as *Our Promised Land* and *River of the West: A Study of Opportunity in the Columbia Empire* and *The Columbia: Powerhouse of the West.*[4] Better known are the products of the decision by the new Bonneville Power Administration in 1941 to hire Woody Guthrie to tour the Bonneville Dam (1937) and Grand Coulee Dam (1941) projects and write celebratory songs. Many Americans have sung the most popular of the compositions Guthrie penned:

Green pastures of plenty from dry barren hills . . .


Roll on, Columbia, roll on.
Your power is turning our darkness to dawn . . .


To white Oregonians in 1957 the drowning of Celilo Falls seemed a regrettable but manageable economic cost and a fascinating example of progress. After all, the four Columbia River fishing tribes — Warm Springs, Yakama, Umatilla, and Nez Perce — shared compensation of $23 million for the loss of fishing sites. Forty years later the flooding of Celilo seems like an ineradicable cultural sin, for no one can reassemble the way of life that revolved around the Falls. There is greater understanding of the sadness of chief Tommy Thompson: "There goes my life. My people will never be the same." Although in 2000 there is active consideration of restoring wild salmon habitat by breaching four smaller Snake River dams on the Columbia's longest tributary, we cannot yet seriously contemplate removing The Dalles Dam itself to uncover the bones of the old cataract.

Portland writers such as Robin Cody in *Ricochet River* and Craig

Bonneville Dam (Oregon Historical Society Neg. 92882). The first of many federal hydroelectric and navigation dams on the Columbia River, Bonneville Dam spans the Columbia Gorge forty miles east of Portland. Its construction triggered intense debate over how and where best to use its cheap electricity. The upshot was a new federal agency, the Bonneville Power Administration, to distribute the power of Bonneville and Grand Coulee on a regional basis. One of the first results was a string of aluminum plants along the lower river that furnished materials for World War II warplanes.

Lesley in *River Song* recognize that the end of fishing at Celilo is now story as well as history—a part of the narrative through which the region understands itself. Poet Earle Thompson wrote about Celilo as "dancing on the rim of the world"—the seam between sky and land, the edge between an old world and a new.[5] Lesley makes the end of the Celilo fishery part of the story that Native Americans transmit from older to younger generation. The end of the falls and the transformation of lifeways stands in for the unbridgeable gaps between fathers and sons, between Danny Kachiah and his father Red Shirt, between Danny and his son Jack. The story is also about the regularity of the old days and the uncertainty of modern America. "They're really helping out those dead Indians," says Jack, the caustic teenager, when Danny describes the relocation of Indian burials from flooded islands to a mass grave behind a ten-foot fence.[6]

Sin may be ineradicable, but it can always be repented. Salmon and their rivers are ubiquitous in public art. Whimsical, realistic, or lyrical, there are salmon on the sides of restaurants and parking garages, at Portland's convention center and along its downtown transit mall. It's a low cost way to remind swarming commuters of a different kind of migration. There are salmon as well in David James Duncan's childhood encounter with Johnson Creek, which flows through the parks and bramble-choked back yards of southeast Portland.

Then I came to water too deep to wade or see the bottom of: a shady black pool, surface-foam eddying like stars in a nebula. . . . I settled, bellydown, on a log, watched the pool; let its foam-starred surface eddy till it became a Van Gogh night sky. I spun and spiraled, grew eddy-headed and foam-dazed, forgot my stars weren't stars. . . . Just as I lost all sense of time, space, creek, sky, rightsideupness and upsideness, up from the sunless depths or down from the foam-starred heavens rose a totem-red totem-green impossibility. Massive, hook-nosed, travel-scarred but clear-eyed. I can think of no better way to describe its indescribable presence than to state the native name: *Coho.*

An old male coho, rising not to eat, as trout do, but just to surface, who knows why. And as it arced up and submarined along it gazed—with one lidless, shining eye—right into me. Gazed not like a fish struggling up from an ocean to die, but like a Tlinget or Kwakiutl messenger dropped down from a realm of deathlessness. The coho sank fast as it had risen, back into the deeps. But not before his unblinking eye changed the way I look out my own.[7]

Some Northwesterners are also defining the relation of people to place in more explicitly religious terms. In May 1999 the region's Roman Catholic hierarchy issued "The Columbia River Watershed: Realities and Possibilities: Reflection in Preparation for a Pastoral Letter." The archbishops of Seattle and Portland and bishops of

CHAPTER 3

Yakima, Spokane, Boise, Helena, Nelson, British Columbia, and Baker City, Oregon explicitly associated stewardship of the river with the Christian imagery of water: the living water Jesus offers to the woman at the well in John 4, the rain of saving grace God sends even to the unjust in Matthew 5, the river of the water of life that flows through the city of God at the end of time.

The Columbia watershed is . . . part of God's creation, transcending humanity's arbitrary political boundaries. The basin is a biologically integrated region having species and habitat needs, interrelated human communities, natural resources to sustain the lives of resident and migrating species, and a splendor that must be conserved. . . .

We, the Canadian and U.S. bishops of the international watershed region . . . offer in this reflection some preliminary suggestions for eliminating problems and eradicating injustices in our common space. We issue this reflection to initiate an ongoing discussion of the needs of the watershed. We propose an integrated spiritual and social vision for the watershed. We hope to encourage attitudes and actions that will help to eliminate harmful policies and practices. We envision a better future in which ecological respect, a spiritual relationship to the rivers and their natural setting, and community renewal will integrally shape our shared environment.

The Columbia watershed should be *sacramental*. The eyes of faith should see signs of the Spirit in this book of nature, signs that complement the understandings of God revealed in the books of the Bible. The Columbia watershed should also be a *commons*: a place shared by all the members of the community of life.

The task of politics is to translate a saving vision into everyday action. The problem, as the name of Oregon's official planning agency puts it, is to balance the claims of "land conservation and development." In practical application the challenge is to shape cities that can prosper without weighing too heavily on the landscape.

To act as stewards of human as well as natural communities,

Portlanders have also tried to develop institutions and policies that integrate individual interests with community interests. Is it possible, for example, to recognize and sustain the distinctive character and values of neighborhoods while linking them to the larger needs of the metropolis? Can institutions and policies span the distances between center city liberals and hillsiders, between everyday suburbanites and aggressive eco-advocates? This story of Portland's efforts to construct an inclusive civic culture and its supporting institutions begins in the 1960s. It builds on racial change, on middle class populist tradition, on strategic leadership, and on new visions of urban and social life. In effect, these questions reverse the approach of Chapter One by asking how Portlanders shape their place.

## PLANNING LIKE A CITY

On August 19, 1969 Riverfront for People held a picnic in the median strip. One midsummer day when the mountains and coast beckoned many Portlanders, two hundred fifty adults and one hundred children spread their blankets and opened their coolers and baskets on a barren strip between four lanes of busy traffic on Front Avenue and an even busier four lanes on Harbor Drive. Riverfront for People organizers Allison and Bob Belcher were there with their kids—aged 18 months and three years—carefully tethered to keep them from straying into traffic. Gretchen and Steve Kafoury, neighbors from across the street in the Irvington neighborhood, were there with daughter Deborah (who thirty years later would follow her parents' political careers to the Oregon legislature). Meeting at nearly the precise spot where pioneers had erected Portland's first buildings, the throng were young and enthusiastic activists who thought that Portland deserved a park along its downtown waterfront.

The trigger for the picnic was the scheduled demolition of a great white elephant—a two-block building constructed in the 1930s as a public market and later used by the *Oregon Journal*. The struc-

Harbor Drive (Oregon Historical Society Neg. 57776). Harbor Drive was part of a major down-town waterfront rehabilitation project of the 1930s. The city replaced rotting wharves and muddy, trash-strewn riverbank with an interceptor sewer and seawall and used the newly filled land behind the wall for a highway bypass around downtown.

ture sat between Front Avenue and Harbor Drive, the latter built around 1940 to divert trucks from downtown retail streets. For high-way engineers, removal opened up the possibility of *more* lanes for *more* traffic. For the hastily organized Riverfront for People, it opened the chance to replace concrete with grass, speeding vehicles with people strolling along the downtown riverfront. The City Club of Portland weighed in with a report that called for "varied public use

. . . and attractive pedestrian access to the esplanade and the river itself."[8] In October the activists achieved their first goal, convincing Glenn Jackson, a utility executive who chaired and ruled the powerful State Highway Commission, that a park was at least a possibility. There were two more years of study and debate before completion of the Fremont Bridge and joining of the inner freeway loop gave traffic an alternative route and allowed the city to rip out Harbor Drive. But it was the activists who introduced the idea, fought off halfway measures (burying Harbor Drive in a tube and topping it with sod was one idea), helped put open-minded leaders on City Council, and deserve the credit for what has grown into Tom McCall Waterfront Park.

If Portland is a nationally recognized "capital of good planning," it is the capital of a small revolution that is epitomized by Riverfront for People. Basic changes in dominant attitudes, plans, and policies originated in a political transformation that began in the neighborhoods in the later 1960s, crested in the 1970s, and continued to develop within the context of new institutions in the 1980s and 1990s. If "revolution" seems too strong a term, let's interrogate the well-known urban affairs journalist Neal Peirce. As late as 1970, he wrote that "if any west coast town could be said to have a monopoly on propriety and an anxiousness to keep things as they are, it is Portland, a town of quiet wealth, discreet culture, and cautious politics." Seventeen years later, answering a query from my colleagues Nancy Chapman and Joan Starker, he described the political climate in Portland as "open, spirited, and of course [ready for] the unconventional."[9]

In the previous generation Portland was nothing to write home about. During the postwar decade city politics revolved around traditional battles between old guard and reformers. Mayor Dorothy Lee (1949–53) started the long process of modernizing a police force that had taken World War II as an opportunity for corruption. A proposal to replace the city commission system of government (adopted in 1913) with a council-manager system, however, stirred interest only from good government aficionados. Voters in 1950 turned down a largely symbolic civil rights ordinance. Public housing and redevelopment plans foundered on the hostility of neighborhoods and the real estate industry.

The drive wheel of politics in the 1950s was a longstanding tension between business interests on the east and west sides of the Willamette River, expressed in bitter electoral battles over the location of public facilities such as a coliseum and domed stadium. The former was built on the "wrong" site at the east end of the Broadway Bridge, despite the best efforts of the downtown establishment to place it in an urban renewal zone south of the central business district. Voters in May and again in November 1964 refused outright to build the "Delta Dome" on the site of Vanport. Unwilling to erect a stadium "on spec" without a commitment from major league baseball, they forfeited the chance to have the country's second domed stadium and probably to acquire expansion baseball and NFL teams (Portland Mariners? Portland Seahawks?).

One reason for introverted battles over issues left over from the 1930s and 1940s was the failure to catch the postwar economic boom. Unlike the aircraft industry in cities such as Los Angeles and Seattle, shipbuilding quickly evaporated. From 1945 to 1965, Portland was stodgy in social tone, cautious in leadership, and stingy with public investments. The neoprogressive political reform movements that spoke for new economic interests and transformed cities such as Denver and Phoenix bypassed Portland. Richard Neuberger, in his days as a journalist before he entered the U.S. Senate, profiled Portland for the *Saturday Evening Post*. What did this eloquent advocate of the New Deal and liberal democracy find most characteristic? "Placidity and gentle living." [10]

In the 1970s, however, Portland experienced radical and remarkable change. Bestriding this political era were Tom McCall as governor from 1967 to 1974 and Neil Goldschmidt as mayor from 1973 to 1979. McCall led through oratory, moral appeal, and political head knocking. Goldschmidt was a master at anticipating common goals and constructing coalitions. Both men inspired political participation and shaped political expectations. But they also depended for success on growing cohorts of activists and on ideas that bubbled up from grassroots advocacy groups. Like the bluffs along the Sandy and Clackamas rivers, they channeled the floods of change.

Part of what happened was a turnover of generations. Civic leadership shifted from men in their sixties and seventies to men and women in their thirties and even twenties. As historian E. Kimbark MacColl has pointed out, there was only 30 percent overlap between lists of the most powerful Portlanders as published in 1969 in the *Labor Press* and the most powerful Oregonians as published in 1975 in the *Oregon Times*. Between 1969 and 1973, the average age on Portland City Council dropped by fifteen years, with similar shifts on the Multnomah County Commission and in the legislative delegation.

The new leaders were men and women whose personal and public consciousness was shaped by the American prosperity of the postwar decades. They came of age through high school, college, and early careers during the great era of American optimism, when economic and political power on the world scene underlay a sense of possibilities at home. They replaced a generation molded for caution by World War I and the Great Depression. Some had been Peace Corps volunteers. Some were experienced in the politics of protest against war in Indochina, turning to reform at the community scale when the Nixon administration rejected and demonized protesters.

A cohort of young activist women added to the ferment. The entry point for many was the 1972 election. Two bright young candidates—Neil Goldschmidt for mayor and Tom Walsh for City Council—mobilized hundreds of volunteers. The day after the election, "the women who had worked on the Goldschmidt campaign met the women who had worked on the Walsh campaign. We met in order to console the Walsh workers and they met to congratulate us.

. . . We met for lunch on Wednesday; decided we liked each other; and decided we should keep doing this."[11] The Wednesday group evolved into Politically Organized Women (POW), who took up the challenge of opening the civic affairs-minded City Club to women. They picketed the club's Friday meetings at the Benson Hotel for two years until the club extended membership.

Generational turnover in Portland politics and the national feminist movement opened more than the City Club. Women like Allison Belcher were tired of entrenched officials telling them, "Don't worry, you're just a housewife."[12] The League of Women Voters and a revitalized Democratic Party offered opportunities to learn and act on public issues. Marjorie Gustafson later recalled that "it was just a wonderful time to be a young woman in Portland. When I talked to my friends in Washington [D.C.], it was clear that people of equal abilities in Washington were worried about the nursery school whereas [my friends] and I were worried about the City of Portland."[13] Out of the overlapping groups of women who discussed politics and policy in each other's living rooms would come members of important appointive boards, state legislators, city and county commission members, and, in the 1990s, Mayor Vera Katz.

The new Portland leadership reflected a changing constituency. Portland was younger in 1970 than it had been in 1950 and 1960. Indeed, the proportion of its residents aged 15–34 increased from 22 to 30 percent during the 1960s. After the slow 1950s, it also began to attract migrants with new energy and ideas, particularly managerial and professional people attracted by new opportunities in finance, services, and electronics. The increase in professional occupations from 12 to 15 percent of the labor force during the 1960s was a good predictor of changing public attitudes.

Portland's new leadership coincided with new ideas in the national dialogue about city planning and politics. Portland's new politics were informed by the national urban renewal and freeway critics of the 1960s. Jane Jacobs, Herbert Gans, and others emphasized the value of small scale and vernacular urban environments and the excitement of large cities. Urban planners rediscovered that downtowns were complex collages of subdistricts rather than unitary wholes. Quality-of-life liberals who worked in the growing information industries and members of minority communities both emphasized the values of place and sought to make neighborhoods effective instruments of resistance to large scale changes in the urban fabric. Within this changing national discourse, Portland stood out not for the content of its vision but for effectiveness in transforming what was becoming a new orthodoxy into a *comprehensive* set of public policies and for constructing long-lived political coalitions around several planning goals.

Portland's remarkable achievements in the 1970s depended on a powerful alliance between downtown business interests and residents of older neighborhoods. Portland had many of the same problems as other cities in the era of "urban crisis." Downtown parking was inadequate, the Rose City Transit Company was bankrupt, and the new Washington Square superregional mall in the affluent western suburbs threatened the end of downtown retailing. At the same time, older neighborhoods were at risk from schemes for large scale land clearance and redevelopment, concentrated poverty, and racial inequities. Many cities understood the situation as a zero sum competition in which downtown businesses and homeowners battled over a fixed pool of resources. Portland is one of the few cities where the "growth machine" business leadership of the 1950s made a graceful transition to participation in a more inclusive political system. We can characterize the resulting political marriage as the mobilization of the open-minded middle.

The chief architect and beneficiary of the political transition was Neil Goldschmidt, a young poverty attorney elected to City Council in 1970 and mayor in 1972, at age thirty-two. He would serve as mayor until he became secretary of transportation in the Carter administration in 1979 and later governor of Oregon in 1987–90. By the start of

Neil Goldschmidt (C. Bruce Forster). Neil Goldschmidt brought new energy and informality to City Hall as city commissioner (1971–72) and mayor (1973–79)

his first mayoral term, Goldschmidt and his staff had drawn on a ferment of political and planning ideas and sketched out an integrated strategy involving the coordination of land use and transportation policies. They were strongly influenced by the 1970 census, which showed the effects of a declining proportion of middle class families on neighborhood diversity and city tax base. During 1973, 1974, and 1975, Goldschmidt's team of young policy specialists and planners brought together a variety of policy initiatives that were waiting for precise definition and articulated them as parts of a single political package that offered benefits for a wide range of citizens and groups.

This so-called "population strategy" emphasized public transportation, neighborhood revitalization, and downtown planning. Better transit would improve air quality, enhance the attractiveness of older neighborhoods, and bring workers and shoppers downtown. In turn, a vital business center would protect property values in surrounding districts and increase their attractiveness for residential reinvestment. Middle class families who remained in or moved into inner neighborhoods would patronize downtown businesses, and prosperity would support high levels of public services. Neighborhood planning would focus on housing rehabilitation and on visible amenities to keep older residential areas competitive with the suburbs.

Preservation of a user friendly downtown was the strategy's cornerstone. Business worries about suburban competition and parking problems coincided at the end of the 1960s with public disgust over a blighted riverfront. The public concern sparked by Riverfront for People in 1969 not only paved (unpaved?) the way for removal of Harbor Drive but also fired imaginations about radical responses to other downtown problems. Richard Ivey, from the planning-engineering firm CH2M-Hill, and City Commissioner Lloyd Anderson introduced the idea of a comprehensive rethinking of downtown. They helped to organize a process by which the younger generation of technically sophisticated citizen activists worked with city officials, downtown retailers, property owners, neighborhood groups, and civic organizations to treat the interrelations of previously isolated issues such as parking, bus service, housing, and retailing. Bob Baldwin, the manager of the planning process, remembered the importance of getting the investors involved: "They were called the Downtown Committee, made up of about thirteen people in the downtown area. We called them the 'Powerful Downtown Committee'. . . . It included some pretty powerful people—the leaders of Portland. Anybody who was a leader who wasn't in this group felt left out, so they wanted to get in." [14]

The Downtown Plan of 1972 offered integrated solutions to a long list of problems that Portlanders had approached piecemeal for two generations. It was technically sound because its proposals were based on improvements in access and transportation. It was politi-

Pioneer Courthouse Square (Livable Oregon, Inc.). Pioneer Courthouse Square replaced a department store parking ramp in the mid-1980s. Bracketed by light rail lines and bordered by the transit mall, it rapidly became a formal and informal gathering place at the most intensively used corners in the city.

cally viable because it prescribed tradeoffs among different interests as part of a coherent strategy. Specifics included new parks and plazas, high density retail and office corridors crossing in the center of downtown, better transit and new parking garages to serve the corridors, districts for special housing incentives, and pedestrian oriented design.

The result is a strong and viable central core that anchors the metropolitan region. Visitors to the city nearly always start at the center. *Time* and the *Atlantic Monthly*, the *Los Angeles Times* and *Architecture*, have all reported on the strength of downtown design, the careful conservation of a sense of place, friendliness to pedestrians, and the enhancement of the downtown with public art. Berton Roueche in the *New Yorker* (1985) pointed to "closely controlled new building, the carefully monitored rehabilitation of worthy old buildings, [and] the vigorous creation of open space" as key factors creating a city of "individuality and distinction." Downtown design earned a City Livability Award from the U.S. Conference of Mayors in 1988 and an Award for Urban Excellence from the Bruner Foundation in 1989.[15]

A not surprising reaction to all this good ink is a skeptical re-characterization of downtown Portland as a Disneylike theme park rather than a "real" place by urban design specialists such as Robert Shibley and Robert Bruegmann. Robert Kaplan's comment is typical: "With its neat trolley lines, geometric parks, rustic flower pots beside polymer-and-glass buildings, crowded sidewalk benches . . . Portland exudes a stagy perfection." [16] The whiteness of Portland's population and its downtown workers and shoppers certainly contributes to the theme park appearance, as does the willingness of many Portlanders actually to use corner trash cans rather than dropping candy wrappers on the curb. Even locals sometimes wonder if we haven't created a toy town rather than a city whose rough edges strike cultural sparks, although it is possible to put a positive spin on Portland as a microcosm of American design. Portland writers Gideon Bosker and Lena Lencek did so in 1985, characterizing it as "an intelligently curated architectural museum . . . a magisterial modern metropolis in which ancient spaces and futuristic skyscraper-sculptures were brought together on miniature, two hundred foot blocks." [17]

Beyond its attractions of place, central Portland has retained economic and institutional dominance in the metropolitan area. The central office core has increased its job total and upgraded average job quality steadily since the 1970s. The number of jobs in five core census tracts increased from 63,000 in 1970 to 108,000 in 1995; jobs in adjacent tracts grew from 40,000 to 50,000.[18] Central Portland claims nearly all the major metropolitan institutions and gathering places: art, history, and science museums, Performing Arts Center and Civic Auditorium, Portland State University and Oregon Health Sciences University, several major hospitals, Civic Stadium, Oregon Convention Center, and Microsoft billionaire Paul Allen's Blazerama (officially the Rose Garden Arena), a new privately funded arena for the Trail Blazers of the NBA. Pioneer Courthouse Square in the heart of the retail core hosts political rallies and community events. Tom McCall Waterfront Park is the place for food-and-fun festivals.

Outside the employment core, Portland lacks the "dead zone" of derelict industrial districts and abandoned neighborhoods that surrounds the high-rise core of many cities. More than forty years ago in 1959, Edgar Hoover and Raymond Vernon (1959) identified the problem of "gray areas" in older cities, the old transitional zones that seemed to be falling out of the real estate market.[19] Since that time, most inner ring districts throughout the United States have followed an up-or-out pattern in which the only options are gentrification or abandonment.

Portland, however, has seen essentially no abandonment and, now, accelerating reinvestment in light industrial and warehousing districts. To use the standard model of urban geography, Portland now treats the downtown core and surrounding frame as a single high density "central city." Downtown Portland is bordered by viable older residential neighborhoods at several income levels and by neighborhoods in the making on abandoned waterfront rail yards and industrial sites. The booming River District on the abandoned Burlington Northern freight yards along the Willamette north of downtown is planned for 5000 units of housing. Redevelopment of a similar riverfront area south of downtown is planned for the next decade.

Several of these adjacent districts were incorporated in the Central City Plan of 1988 rather than excluded as irrelevant to a growing downtown. An update of the 1972 plan, the Central City Plan identified which downtown areas to appropriate for intensified development for information industries and workers and which to stabilize for blue collar jobs. An innovative industrial sanctuary policy uses a zoning overlay to protect inner manufacturing and warehousing districts in Northwest Portland and the central east side from incompatible uses such as big box retailing. This industrial sanctuary policy is a powerful tool for avoiding the mismatch between the location of jobs and housing that afflicts many metropolitan areas. In effect, the plan and policy recognize that a seaport and regional trade center needs to push both paper and payloads.

One reason Portland is so strong at the center is the lack of a suburban beltway. In the 1950s, highway engineers decided to bring the city's first limited access freeways into the center of the city and connect them with a tight freeway loop that hugged the edges of the central business district. As an engineering decision, the route took advantage of available or easily acquired rights of way and avoided the steepest parts of the West Hills. The inner freeway made it possible to remove Harbor Drive in favor of Waterfront Park; it helped maintain downtown Portland and its nearby neighborhoods as the most accessible parts of the metropolitan area after the demise of streetcars and interurban railways. A suburban freeway bypass through the less fashionable eastern half of the metropolitan area did not open until the 1980s. Plans for a southwestern quadrant in the 1990s stalled in political traffic, and a northwestern quadrant that would violate parks and open spaces and require multiple bridges across the Columbia River is even less likely, leaving the metro area with only half a beltway.

Outside the urban core, Goldschmidt's second goal was to recycle older neighborhoods that had been built from the 1880s through the 1930s. The city used federal Housing and Community Development Block Grant funds and leveraged private capital with tax free borrowing for an extensive housing rehabilitation program. Inflation of suburban housing costs in the 1970s and again in the 1990s also helped retain families in older, affordable neighborhoods. Several neighborhoods between the downtown and the base of the West Hills — Corbett, Lair Hill, Goose Hollow, and Northwest — experienced gradual gentrification by new residents looking for Portland's closest facsimile of a sophisticated urban environment.

The bungalow belt on the east side of the Willamette attracted a new generation of Portlanders wanting traditional city neighborhoods of 50-by-100-foot lots, trees, sidewalks, and stores within walking distance.

Together, such neighborhoods became the homeland of progressive Portland and voted increasingly for Goldschmidt's allies and heirs in city government and for liberal Democrats for the state legislature. An example is the Irvington-Alameda-Grant Park district in northeast Portland—Henry and Ramona's neighborhood—which entered the revolutionary era firmly in the moderate Republican camp. The district was liberal on its lower cost edges and increasingly conservative as houses grew larger toward the center. Democrat Jane Cease, with a background as president of the League of Women Voters, ran unsuccessfully for the district's seat in the Oregon House of Representatives in 1974 and 1976 before breaking through in 1978. Her campaigns drew on neighborhood activists, politically oriented women, young liberal Democrats, and voters "organized on a block level to get out the vote" for a school funding measure in 1968. In recent decades the district has grown more solidly Democratic and liberal.[20]

A political bargain with neighborhood activists accompanied direct investment policy. After a series of testy confrontations about zoning and land development between neighborhoods and City Hall in the late 1960s, the new Goldschmidt administration decided to legitimize and partially coopt neighborhood activists by incorporating independent neighborhood associations as secondary participants in public decision making. Mary Pedersen, staff for the very active Northwest District Association, helped write the ordinance: "I had concluded that unless there was staff organized into an office (we all hated the word bureau), then the neighbors would not have the support they needed to get across their message to city bureaus and specifically, the planning office. . . . We had really argued with great energy to City Council that we needed to be independent of the agency that was responsible for so much planning and got the distrust that resulted from top-down planning." [21]

The city's Office of Neighborhood Associations (now the Office of Neighborhood Involvement) was established in 1974 with Pedersen as its first director. It provides city funds for neighborhood association activities and monitors their conduct for openness, but does not dictate issues or positions. The acceptance and financial support of voluntary neighborhood groups has offered a *partial* alternative both to confrontational tactics from the grassroots and to top-down management of citizen participation from City Hall.

The third element of the strategy was to shift investment from highways to public transit. As was happening around the nation, a new Tri-County Metropolitan Transit District (Tri-Met) absorbed the bankrupt bus system in 1969. A key feature of the Downtown Plan was a transit mall that drew on the experience of Minneapolis. Completed in 1978, the mall dedicated two north-south streets through the heart of downtown to buses, increasing the speed of service and facilitating transfers. Buses along the mall and elsewhere within the inner freeway loop are free. "Fareless Square" allows Portland's elongated downtown to function as a single district.

Another major transit decision was the 1975 cancellation of the so-called Mount Hood Freeway, Portland's own contribution to the freeway revolt that was sweeping American cities. The five-mile connector expressway between I-5 in the center of Portland and I-205 through the eastern suburbs would have devastated half a dozen lower middle class neighborhoods in southeast Portland. Again, the freeway action was the result of a downtown-neighborhood alliance. The self-interest of neighborhoods in the path of the freeway was obvious. At the same time, a significant segment of downtown businesses were convinced that centrally focused public transit would be more beneficial than a second eastside radial freeway. Most of the federal money was transferred to build a successful fifteen-mile light rail line from downtown to the eastern suburb of Gresham. In the mid-1990s, Tri-Met's radial bus and rail system carried 30 to 35 percent of the workers who commute into downtown Portland (roughly twice the proportion in Phoenix or Salt Lake City). In contrast, the count of automobiles entering and leaving downtown was stable from 1987 to 1997.

The openness of civic life in Portland is the basis for an emphasis on team play. Public life takes place around a big table. Some of the seats are reserved for elected officials and heavy hitters from the business community. But anyone can sit in who accepts the rules (politeness is important) and knows how to phrase ideas in the language of middle class policy discussion (the goal is to do "what's good for the city"). Once an organization or interest group is at the table, or on the team, it has an opportunity to shape policy outcomes.

Even the volatile issues of low income housing and services for the homeless have been handled through consensus policies. Advocates for homeless persons and lower income households have certainly had to battle for attention in City Hall and downtown board rooms. However, the Portland style is to bring into the conversation "well-behaved" advocacy groups that have gained attention. Once at the table, such groups can trade acquiescence with long term land redevelopment goals for substantial public commitments to low income housing and social services.

A few representative examples show the process at work. In the 1980s, agencies serving the homeless population of Portland's skid road agreed to a cap on shelter beds in the Burnside/Old Town district in return for a go-slow approach to redevelopment and an active program for relocating shelters and social services. A charismatic advocate for the homeless who declined to sign on found that contributions quickly dried up while newspapers headlined his own flaws of character and abusive behavior. In contrast, the Northwest Pilot Project monitors the loss of low cost downtown housing and repeatedly chides the city for neglecting the poor in its plans for a

"Three Women, Starlight Parade" (Lawrence Shlim, gelatin silver print, 1992, Visual Chronicle of Portland). The image of downtown Portland as a tidy middle class theme park (a homemade version of Universal Studio Citywalk, perhaps) is belied by the continued presence of residents on the economic margin. The retirees in "Three Women, Starlight Parade," a photograph by Lawrence Shlim, are watching one of the two big events of the annual Rose Festival.

bright new downtown, but it also works within the framework of Portland progressivism to build coalitions among government, foundations, businesses, and social service agencies. In 1995, the Portland Organizing Project forced consideration of low income housing as a component of the River District north of downtown. Once the development leadership recognized the power of POP's populist appeal, however, they moved rapidly to enfold low income housing and its more consensus-minded advocates into the planning process (leaving POP on the outside and favoring the somewhat poor over the very poor). Also in downtown is the Outside-In clinic and drop-in center for street youth. Its roots lie in the alternative organizations of the 1970s, but it recently agreed to share county funding with "tougher" business backed agencies, with each carving its special niche. In the Portland context, all of these easily multiplied cases are seen as inclusiveness rather than cooptation.

The Goldschmidt strategy has so far enjoyed nearly a three-decade run. Mayor Frank Ivancie (1981–84), who had worked as executive assistant to Goldschmidt's predecessor, pushed for more traditional redevelopment, but accomplished little during years of economic recession. The political alliance has been maintained by mayors Bud Clark (1985–92) and Vera Katz (1993- ). It has been supported by a majority of the four city commissioners and many members of the Multnomah County Commission, many of whom tend to compete for the mantle of progressive innovator and consensus builder.

Despite political consensus, not everyone in the city is happy, for it is difficult to promote infill and intensification without disrupting and angering neighborhoods. Middle class communities

"Mayor Bud Clark in His Office, Portland, OR or Re: Expose" (Stu Levy, gelatin silver print, 1990, Visual Chronicle of Portland). Bud Clark, a neighborhood activist and small business owner, was a surprise winner in the 1984 mayoral election. The victory represented the voters' preference for middle class progressivism over the hard-edged managerial style of incumbent Frank Ivancie. This photographic print by Stu Levy represents something of Clark's exuberant personality.

dislike the loss of single family character when row houses and apartments pop up along transit streets. Aging hippies fear that Portland's pleasant funkiness will be yuppied out. Lower status neighborhoods fear both unaffordable upscaling and the return of the riffraff they've worked so hard to eliminate from stable family communities. These neighborhoods have struggled to maintain their viability in the face of suburbanization, institutional disinvestment, and sometimes public neglect even while middle class Portland was thriving. A beauty salon proprietor resents the possibility of gentrifiers along a planned light rail extension: "Martha Stewart doesn't live here. This is North Portland. We are blue-collar, hardworking people. We like the neighborhood the way it is. The planners don't understand that."[22] Other residents worry that higher densities in "town centers" and along "main street" transit corridors under the Region 2040 Plan (see below) will mean new low income renters who will pull them back just as they have fought off urban decay—renters who will be "tucked neatly away . . . out of sight from the rest of Portland," as one North Portland neighborhood activist complains.[23] Residents of low income Lents in outer southeast Portland are eager for redevelopment funds but wonder whether the city's plans for infill will irrevocably alter their low density community.[24]

Part of the problem is a focus on numerical targets rather than design, on the location of the Urban Growth Boundary (UGB, described more fully in the next section) rather than what happens inside. Legislation that the homebuilders helped lobby through Salem in the early 1990s turned a planning goal of a twenty-year supply of land within the Urban Growth Boundary into a statutory requirement. Under pressure to focus on numbers rather than neighbors, planning agencies have moved from the 2040 concept to specific zoning changes without the intermediate step of community visioning. Where that step has been taken, residents have been strongly supportive of increased density—such as plans for 4–5-story redevelopment in the Hollywood neighborhood commercial center that developed between 1920 and 1950.

As this example suggests, infill and redevelopment face the challenges of good design. Neighbors want new construction that feels compatible—not row houses perched on huge garages. Portland City Council in 2000 notoriously prohibited new garage-front "snout houses" ("In Portland, Houses Are Friendly. Or Else" read the *New York Times* headline).[25] Builders complain that the prohibition is one more restriction that unnecessarily raises the cost of new housing, and other critics wonder whether it is possible to get quality infill without stifling overregulation. The answer seems to be yes, as shown by the growing number and quality of entries for the fifth year of the Governor's Livability Awards. Winners in Portland neighborhoods include both owner occupied and rental units that are affordable and compatible with their surroundings.

Friends of streams and trees also have grounds for complaint. The mid-1990s brought a rising awareness within the city of Portland that increased housing density will consume informal open spaces and vacant lands—those weedy lots where kids play and the wooded slopes that used to be too steep for development. With thousands of new housing units expected inside the city limits, many residents fear that there will be no breathing space, no rest for the eye. The development of surplus park land in the St. Johns neighborhood (a section of North Portland known for its independence, working class pride, and justified complaints about neglect from City Hall) has pitted the grassroots organizing goal of neighborhood stability against the metropolitan environmental agenda of limiting sprawl. People in the middle class neighborhood of Multnomah in Southwest Portland fought plans to put row houses on vacant acres because of perceived threats to the neighborhood's cozy, countrified character.

In fact, the Portland region is making deliberate choices about its types and locations of open space. Regional growth plans imply infill of vacant lots and empty parcels. The Portland area has numerous large parks and extensive stream corridors close to its center (urban coyotes and suburban cougars that share these spaces became a public concern in the 1990s). In addition, voters in 1995 gave Metro a $136 million bond issue to acquire potential park lands both inside and outside the heavily urbanized area. In broadest terms, the compact city model trades off neighborhood open space for quicker access to rural lands outside the metropolitan area.

The buried issue is not so much the amount of open space as its accessibility by socioeconomic class. As their taxes pay off Metro's bonds, Portlanders will be buying suburban parks and preserves. As they cope with infill housing, they will be protecting farms and forested hillsides fifteen miles away. Metro by June 2000 had acquired 5763 acres for regional trails, greenways, natural reserves, and parks. Such spaces are great for hikers, mountain bikers, and weekend excursions. They are less useful for inner neighborhood kids and summer youth programs.

## THINKING LIKE A METROPOLIS

No moment looms larger in the legend of modern Oregon than Governor Tom McCall's rousing land use speech in January 1973. "There is a shameless threat to our environment and to the whole quality of life — the unfettered despoiling of the land," he told the state legislature. He pointed an outraged finger at malefactors in the best style of Theodore Roosevelt. "Sagebrush subdivisions, coastal condomania, and the ravenous rampage of suburbia in the Willamette Valley all threaten to mock Oregon's status as the environmental model for the nation. . . . The interests of Oregon for today and in the future must be protected from grasping wastrels of the land."[26]

The language was judgmental and personalized. Here was no inevitable process of land conversion driven by an impersonal market. Like a latter day Amos or Jeremiah, McCall knew sinners when he saw them. With the ringing tones of the Old Testament, his prophetic rhetoric targeted aberrant behavior ("condo*mania*") by miscreants ("grasping wastrels"). He invoked moral standards that in a right world would cause evildoers to feel *shame* for their actions. Like Neil Goldschmidt in Portland, McCall claimed and articulated ideas that were already in ferment around Oregon—bottle deposits, protection of public access to Pacific beaches, a Willamette River Greenway. His gift was less the ability to devise new policies than the political acumen to sell such ideas to the public—and by so doing, to the legislature.

For students of metropolitan politics, Portland offers textbook examples of innovation in regional planning and government. Created in the 1970s and tested by rapid growth in the 1990s, both Oregon's statewide system for land use planning—McCall's legacy—and Metro, the nation's only elected regional government, had their origins in the 1950s and 1960s. They derive from both moralistic politics and the incremental evolution of bureaucratic institutions.

Metro's beginnings are in 1957, the year of Sputnik and those extravagant Chevrolet tail fins. The seed was the Metropolitan Planning Commission, a rudimentary Council of Governments established so the Portland area could get its share of federal funds for regional planning. The Metropolitan Planning Commission prepared the first regionwide base maps and land use inventory, but (of course) none of the city or county governments really wanted it to *plan*.

Ten years later, this weak organization evolved into CRAG (Columbia Region Association of Governments). The study committee that pushed the change had originally wanted a federated municipality on the model of Miami-Dade County or Metro Toronto. When they discovered that support in the legislature was zero, the fallback position was a standard council of governments for five area counties and thirty-one municipalities. CRAG had all the problems common to COGs. Funding was a precarious combination of federal grants and contributions from member governments. Like the United States with the United Nations, cities and counties forgot to send the check when they got peeved. Suburban jurisdictions were particularly concerned that CRAG not turn into the mouthpiece of Portland under Neil Goldschmidt's strong leadership. Nevertheless, CRAG survived a statewide referendum in 1976 that would have abolished all councils of government in Oregon.

A crisis in the delivery of regional services had already incited a burst of institutional creativity. In 1969–70, the metropolitan area got three new regional service agencies. One was Tri-Met, to rescue the failing bus system. The second was the Port of Portland, to consolidate the operation of marine terminals and airports. The third was a Metropolitan Service District (MSD), a governmental "box" that could hold as many service responsibilities as voters or the legislature were willing to assign to it. Depending on regional politics, it had the potential to be an empty shell or a powerful operating agency. Regional voters approved MSD in May 1970, but the agency started small. It planned for regional solid waste disposal (with a tiny budget from a tax on used tires), and it took over the Washington Park Zoo, a Portland-owned facility that needed major new investment. Portland handed it off to MSD in 1976 so that improvements could be made with a *regional* bond issue.

The big change came in 1978. The National Academy for Public Administration passed on HUD money for a study of multilevel government reorganization. The resulting proposal was to merge CRAG's planning functions into the Metropolitan Service District (because the latter had a legal status that was firmly fixed by statute and by explicit voter approval in 1970) and change governance to an elected council. The study commission took very seriously the complaint that local officials who also serve at the area-wide level (as in COGs) are forced to walk an impossibly fine line between regional

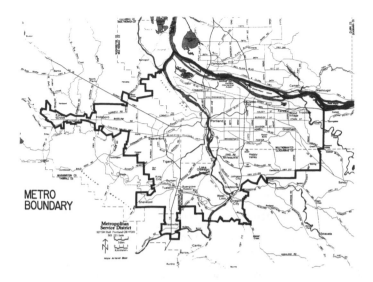

METRO
BOUNDARY

Metro boundary map (Metro). The boundaries of Metro were set by legislation and voter approval in 1978. It covers the contiguous urbanized area of Multnomah, Clackamas, and Washington Counties. Metro's fixed jurisdictional boundary is not identical with the flexible Urban Growth Boundary that Metro administers.

solutions and the demands of the local community they were elected to represent. Direct election of the regional governing body, said its report, was "the best, and perhaps only, way to secure a democratic, responsive, responsible and effective area-wide government." [27]

An analogy from American history backed the argument. The CRAG and MSD boards of the 1970s were similar to the ineffectual national Congress under the Articles of Confederation of 1778–89. Congressional delegates under the Articles represented states rather than citizens. The failure of the Articles had led to the adoption of the federal Constitution, under which members of Congress directly represent individual citizens. If the Constitution had been a good idea, so was a new Metro, said its advocates.

Metro began with power divided between its council and a separately elected executive officer, a setup intended to give the latter a political base to stand up to strong mayors and county commissioners. In November 2000 voters amended the charter to provide for six councilors elected by districts, a council president elected at large, and an appointed administrator.

Area voters went to the polls in May 1978 and said yes to the new idea, although a ballot title that began "Abolish CRAG . . ." has always left a lingering question whether voters knew precisely what they voted for. Since 1978, the new and improved Metropolitan Service District (now officially pared down to "Metro") has grown up. In 1990 voters statewide approved a constitutional amendment allowing Metro to function under a home rule charter. Two years later area voters adopted just such a charter. In effect, this was the fifth vote for regional government in two decades. The charter retained the independently elected executive, set the number of councilors at seven, restated Metro's broad service mandate, and clarified and strengthened planning powers.

Metro now serves roughly 1.3 million people in the urbanized areas of Multnomah, Clackamas, and Washington Counties (the fringes of the counties lie outside its boundaries). It is responsible for regional solid waste planning and disposal. It operates the Oregon Zoo and the former Multnomah County park system and is in the process of acquiring thousands of acres of future parks and open space reserves. Through a semi-independent Metropolitan Exposition-Recreation Commission it oversees the Oregon Convention Center, the downtown Performing Arts Center, and several lesser regional entertainment and convention facilities. Public transit remains under Tri-Met, and municipalities and special districts provide water and sewer service.

Although Portlanders benefit from these services, they are more likely to think of Metro as a planning agency whose authority carries implications for every jurisdiction in its territory. Metro is designated as the metropolitan planning organization (MPO) for the allocation of federal transportation funds. It is also the agency that defined the Portland area Urban Growth Boundary under the Oregon land use planning system, and the agency responsible for periodically re-viewing and redefining that boundary. Finally, Metro has the charter-based responsibility to define regional planning goals and guide-lines that are binding on cities and counties.

The context for Portland area planning, including the Urban Growth Boundary, is Oregon's state system of land use planning, the second key institution that sets Portland apart from other metro-politan areas. In 1973 the legislature established a mandatory plan-ning program administered by a state Land Conservation and Devel-opment Commission (LCDC). The legislation, usually referenced as Senate Bill 100, has survived numerous legal challenges and three statewide referenda. It requires every Oregon city and county to pre-pare a comprehensive plan that responds to a set of statewide goals. The plans provide the legal support for zoning and other specific regulations, and the LCDC can require local governments to revise plans that do not conform to the state goals. Oregon thus operates with a system of strong local planning carried on within enforceable state guidelines that express a vision of the public interest.

In both its origins and its continued political strength, the Ore-gon planning system represents another persistent coalition that spans rural and urban economic interests in the Willamette Valley. The original goal of Oregon Trail emigrants, the valley contains the state's richest farmland, its three largest cities of Portland, Salem, and Eugene, and 70 percent of its population. The movement for state mandated planning originated in efforts by Willamette Valley farmers to protect their livelihoods and communities from urban en-gulfment and scattershot subdivisions, with their disruptive effects on agricultural practices. Republican legislator Hector Macpherson of Linn County recalled that "at the time, I was a dairy farmer ter-ribly concerned with what was happening around me, because of the houses moving in around me out there."[28] As the effort moved through several legislative versions between 1970 and 1973, fear of California style sprawl and the possibility of a mini-megalopolis in the Eugene-Seattle corridor attracted Willamette Valley urbanites to the legislative coalition.

Governor Tom McCall brought together the different constituencies in some practical politicking after the January 1973 speech. He was not only a prophet but a skilled deal maker. He helped cement the legislative alliance that had been started by Macpherson and Portland's liberal Democrat Ted Hallock. He appointed special committees to bang heads, twist arms, and hammer out legislation acceptable to resource businesses and the construction industry. The final land use measure that emerged from the back rooms drew overwhelming legislative support from all parts of the Valley—and very little initial support from eastern Oregon or the coast, whose residents worried about lack of development rather than an excess.

From the start, the statewide goals linked older urban planning concerns to a newer environmentalism. The LCDC program rapidly evolved from a purely reactive effort to fend off erosion of the state's farm economy to a positive attempt to shape a particular urban form. Several goals have been of special importance for directing metropolitan growth—Goal 3 on the preservation of farmland, Goal 5 on the preservation of open space, Goal 10 on access to affordable housing, Goal 11 on the orderly development of public facilities and services, Goal 13 on energy efficient land use, and Goal 14 on the definition of Urban Growth Boundaries (UGBs) to separate urbanizable from rural lands. Although very different in origins from Portland's *city* planning initiatives, the state program thus ended up blending the interests and combining the votes of urbanists, agriculturalists, and environmental advocates in a way that has mirrored and supported the similar alliance at the metropolitan scale. The Oregon Farm Bureau Federation, environmental activists, and Portland politicians have all remained strong supporters for twenty-five years.

Metro adopted the Urban Growth Boundary for the Portland area in 1979 after five years of staff work and hearings. Supposedly providing a twenty-year supply of developable land, the UGB embraced 236,000 acres (369 square miles). Outlying metropolitan communities such as St. Helens and Newberg have their own UGBs. The intent is to prevent sprawl by providing for "an orderly and efficient transition from rural to urban use." Within the UGB, the burden of proof rests on opponents of land development. Outside the boundary, the burden rests on developers to show that their land is easily supplied with necessary services, that it has little worth as resource land or farmland, and that adequate land for the proposed development does not exist within the UGB. The UGBs around Portland and the other Willamette Valley cities have created a dual land market that assigns different values to acreage inside and outside the boundary.[29]

The UGB is coupled with Goal 10, which mandates a mild "fair share" housing policy by requiring that every jurisdiction within the UGB provide "appropriate types and amounts of land . . . necessary and suitable for housing that meets the housing needs of households of all income levels." In other words, suburbs are not allowed to use the techniques of exclusionary zoning to block apartment construction or to isolate themselves as islands of large lot zoning, as decided by court cases involving the suburbs of Milwaukie and Happy Valley. By limiting the speculative development of large, distant residential tracts, the LCDC system has tended to level the playing field for suburban development and discourage the emergence of suburban "super developers" with overwhelming political clout. In the Portland region, a Housing Rule adopted by LCDC now requires that every jurisdiction zone at least half of its vacant residential land for attached single family housing or apartments. By 1998 and 1999, 50 percent of new housing starts in the region were apartments and attached dwellings, up from 35 percent in 1992–95. In effect, the rule enacts a soft version of a fair share program that hopes to reduce socioeconomic disparities between city and suburbs by manipulating density and urban form.[30]

LCDC has also adopted a Transportation Rule that requires local jurisdictions in the metropolitan area to plan land uses and facilities to achieve a 10 percent *reduction* in vehicle miles traveled per capita by 2016 and 15 percent by 2026. The rule flies in the face of the explosive nationwide growth of automobile mileage per capita. It requires a drastic rethinking of land use patterns and transportation investment to encourage mixed uses, higher densities, public transit, and pedestrians. It makes local land use planners and the Oregon Department of Transportation into allies at the same time that the federal Intermodal Surface Transportation Enhancement Act has pushed highway builders to rethink their jobs.

Within these frameworks, a logical expansion of the Goldschmidt coalition and the Mount Hood Freeway bargain was the definition of a common transportation agenda by the City of Portland and key suburban cities around plans for a four-spoke light rail system. Over the objections of weakly organized suburban manufacturers who prefer cross-suburb road improvements, the Portland area's civic leadership in the later 1980s decided that strong public transit should be an axiom of regional development. The cities of Gresham to the east and Hillsboro and Beaverton to the west recognized that light rail links to downtown Portland offer strong development potential for secondary activity centers. With visions of Walnut Creek, California and Bethesda, Maryland glimmering in the future, leaders in these communities have chosen to pursue a role as outlying anchors on radial transportation lines rather than as beads on a beltway. In the words of Beaverton Mayor Rob Drake in 1997, "What's good for Beaverton is good for Portland. And vice versa."[31]

The region's light rail system (MAX, for Metropolitan Area Express) began with the east side line in 1986. An eighteen-mile west side line opened in 1998 with an impressively deep and costly tunnel through the West Hills. A north-south line has been problematic, however. Voters in the three Oregon counties approved a line from Clackamas County through downtown Portland and across the

Light rail (Livable Oregon, Inc.). A light rail train passes Pioneer Courthouse Square, the center point for the east side line, completed in the 1980s, and the west side line, built in the 1990s.

Columbia to Clark County in 1995, but rejection by Clark County voters forced the project back on the ballot. Despite the argument of *The Oregonian* that light rail is essential for "Oregon's environmentally wise anti-sprawl policy,"[32] voters statewide rejected a state contribution to an Oregon-only north-south line in 1996 (in spite of attached sweeteners of highway projects around the state). Tricounty voters narrowly rejected a local financing package for a north line in 1998. It is unclear whether the troubles of north-south light rail represent the fracture of the city-suburb coalition or a combination of discrete factors: fallout from political infighting in Clackamas County, general anti-spending sentiment, downstate response to environmentally oriented ballot measures that could be read as antirural, second thoughts about the efficiency of rail transit investment, transit advocates unhappy with a half measure—or all of the above. However, a spur line to the airport is going forward using money from the city, Tri-Met, airline fees, and a substantial private contribution from the Bechtel Corporation, which owns an industrial park along the line. In addition, a scaled down six-mile North Port-

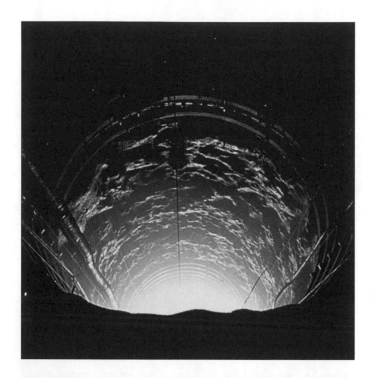

"Westside Light Rail #8" (Patrick Stearns, gelatin silver print, 1995, Visual Chronicle of Portland). The west side light rail project of the 1990s was far more complex than the east side project of the 1980s. Engineers decided to deal with the barrier of the West Hills by driving a pair of three-mile tunnels that run up to 320 feet below the surface. This photograph by Patrick Stearns shows a section of the tube under construction in 1995.

land line is likely to be built without requiring voter approval of new bonds or taxes.

With the state LCDC system as a framework, Portlanders since the early 1990s have also engaged in a prolonged and intelligent debate about metropolitan growth and form. Metro staff in 1988 realized that there was no established process for amending the Portland area Urban Growth Boundary, even though the state requires periodic review and anticipates incremental UGB expansion. A reviving economy and fast-rising in-migration made the task more urgent. The agency undertook a "Region 2040" plan for up to a million more residents in the four core counties. The process included homebuilders and commercial real estate interests as well as growth management advocates. It was also remarkable for actually changing ideas, starting as an effort to figure out how much to expand the UGB and ending with a debate over how best to constrain its expansion.

The UGB has even attracted the attention of artists, surely a rarity for a land use regulation. Dancer and performance artist Linda K. Johnson in 1999 set up camp for thirty-six-hour stints at six different points on the growth boundary, living in a tent supplied with a TV set and Martha Stewart dishes and bedding. She quickly replaced her specialized choreography with straightforward chats with visitors, pulling opinions from yuppies, school kids, construction workers, and architects. Out of the resulting "suburban still life" came new, complex understandings of the way that the UGB has affected

Linda at Cedar Hills (Yalcin Erhan). Linda Johnson poses at the Urban Growth Boundary in Washington County as part of her performance series "Spanning Boundaries: The View from Here." By spending 36 hours at each of six sites along the UGB—"finding, marking and living on the line"—Johnson gave tangible form to the invisible divide between city and country.

"every single solitary aspect of the way we live ... traffic, education, taxes, our desires about housing and architecture." For Johnson— and for many other Portlanders—the growth boundary has become "a different viewfinder to see the city through." [33]

Poet Judith Berck also mused on the visual and conceptual tensions of the UGB in "Driving Portland's Urban Growth Boundary."

Left side of the road stands a skeleton,

steel beams in a big box, every second another bolt for strength, going up

a building for minds that build machines for minds

propped up by much yen and a thousand white-shirted hopes.

Right side of the road a skeleton still stands, brown rotted beams at all
    angles,

closer to earth after every storm, going down

pressing against tall grasses,

once a house for mares, black goats and a summer's worth of hay.

You can see through the ribs to filbert trees and asparagus bolted wild,

pushed into earth by hands and now skeletons.

I drive between receding and arriving.[34]

The Metro Council adopted the Region 2040 Growth Concept in December 1994, outlining broad spatially defined goals for accommodating anticipated growth over the next half century. The document matches the national professional belief in compact cities by proposing to focus new jobs and housing on downtown Portland, urban and suburban centers, and transportation corridors; by identifying rural reserves to remain permanently outside the UGB (including farm and forest land and prominent natural features); and by adapting transportation improvements to the land use goals. The 2040 plan anticipates sharply increased population density in central Portland, in six regional growth centers, and along transit corridors.

Metro followed with two further bureaucratic steps. In October 1996 it adopted an Urban Growth Management Functional Plan to allocate nearly half a million new residents and jobs anticipated by 2017 *within* the Urban Growth Boundary. In turn, the goals of the functional plan are part of a charter-mandated comprehensive Regional Framework Plan that Metro adopted in December 1997. Under Metro's 1992 charter, local jurisdictions must modify their own zoning and land use regulations to implement "functional plans."[35] Among them, Gresham, Hillsboro, and Beaverton anticipate 47,000 new housing units and Portland anticipates 70,000, a vivid demonstration of the strength of the city-suburb coalition around compact growth. In December 1998 the agency met a state deadline by bringing 3500 more acres inside the UGB, although subsequent court decisions have reopened the question of whether all 3500 acres are the right acres. Metro estimates that the expansion will accommodate 23,000 houses and apartments and 14,000 jobs. It added another 377 acres in 1999.

Census data on the amount of densely developed land suggest that the UGB is working. Between 1950 and 1970—the first two decades of unimpeded automobile suburbanization—the area of urbanized land exploded while the average population density fell by a third. From 1970 to 1980, the subdivision frontier continued its rapid expansion but the decline in average density slowed markedly. Since the Urban Growth Boundary was put into place in 1979, the area of developed land has increased much more slowly and the downward trend in average residential density actually reversed. From 1980 to 1994, the metropolitan population increased by 25 percent but the land devoted to urban uses increased only 16 percent. In contrast, population in the Chicago area rose 4 percent from 1970 to 1990 but urbanized land by 46 percent. In 1994 the Portland area was building new housing at a density of 5 dwelling units per acre. By 1998 the density of new development averaged 8 dwellings per acre, actually exceeding the 2040 Plan target. The average new lot size in 1998 was 6200 square feet, down from 12,800 square feet in 1978.[36]

Just as downtown Portland can be viewed as a living museum of contemporary development projects, neighborhoods and suburbs in the 1990s were becoming an open air catalog of the neotraditional planning associated with architects Andres Duany, Peter Calthorpe, and other members of the Congress for the New Urbanism. In older districts there are examples of successful infill with blocks of new apartments over retail space along transit streets. On the east side is Fairview Village, a neotraditional development with single family houses on small lots, commercial-civic center, and dedicated pedestrians and bike paths. On the west side, Orenco Station is a prime example of planning for intensive use around light rail stops; at build-out it will have 436 single family houses, 1400 apartments, a town center, and loft apartments over retail establishments. Time will tell how many such developments the currently strong market will absorb.

Despite rapid building and neotraditional experiments, Portland in the late 1990s was a tight housing market for new households and working class families. In the aggregate, housing prices rose rapidly in the 1970s, dropped during Oregon's prolonged recession in the early and middle 1980s, but recovered and escalated rapidly in the 1990s. In constant dollars, the median sale price of a single family house in the Portland area increased by 50 percent from 1988 to 1995, finally passing the previous high of 1979, according to Harvard's Joint Center for Housing Studies.[37] Housing prices continued to rise rapidly for the next several years, but slowed in 1999 and 2000.

A tight housing market has also brought new buyers to previously undervalued neighborhoods. In the early 1990s, middle class neighborhoods on the less fashionable east side of Portland closed much of the price gap with west side neighborhoods. By the mid-

1990s, families and speculators were hunting for rapidly disappearing bargains in neglected working class and racially mixed areas. Commented one retired grocery checker from northeast Portland to an *Oregonian* reporter, "That's the talk of the town, people coming over and buying up these houses. You look at all the people. They're not black. I thought you people were too scared to come over in this neighborhood."[38]

Advocates of growth management and proponents of untrammeled markets can agree on many facts but not the cause. The Metropolitan Home Builders Association and market advocates argue that a tight Urban Growth Boundary artificially constricts land supply and drives up the price of undeveloped land, with serious consequences for home prices. Growth managers, and Metro in specific, think that the essential problem is one of booming demand as Portland enjoys flush times and what may be a one time influx of capital from a wave of California in-migrants in the early 1990s, creating a speculative "bump" in the housing market. They cite Urban Land Institute data that price increases for residential building lots in Portland for 1990–95 were in line with increases in numerous comparable cities from Albuquerque to Indianapolis to Charlotte; the increase in the later 1990s was less than in unbounded cities such as Denver, Phoenix, and Salt Lake City. An analysis by Bay Area Economists in 1999 noted that housing prices in Portland were still below those in most other west coast metropolitan areas, suggesting that competing metropolitan housing markets have been moving toward equilibrium. Believers in a compact Portland also argue that expansion of the UGB would be a temporary fix at best, with much land freed by such an expansion being used for large lot developments. Using the national literature on the costs of sprawl, they argue that a compact city promotes affordability by reducing infrastructure costs and by encouraging small lot development, infill, and accessory units.[39]

There is little doubt that maintaining a tight growth boundary maintains the equity of working class homeowners by interrupting the classic trickle-down approach to affordable housing. Traditionally we have assumed that the housing market operates like a big thrift shop. Upper income families in search of newer and bigger houses will walk away from perfectly good though somewhat worn neighborhoods and hand them down the economic ladder. This process has made some affordable housing available, but it has also tended to devalue working class neighborhoods except when aggregate demand is very high. Indeed, the trickle-down model has seriously undercut homeownership as a capital accumulation strategy for the working class. With a tight UGB, the Portland area will be less likely to hand down cheap housing for new households, but also less likely to undermine the investments of many working class and middle class families.

Behind the competing evaluations are alternative analytical premises and different visions of the good city. Market arguments against UGBs (and also against light rail) are generic and theory based, asserting that "this is how IT works." Such arguments have become more prominent as Portland has absorbed more outsiders without "Oregon" values. Defenders of the "Portland way" stress the importance of local circumstances and the special validity of place; they will deny, for example, that Portland would ever make the disastrous disinvestment in bus service that damaged Los Angeles in the 1990s. Remembering that households rent or buy a neighborhood as well as a dwelling unit with each housing choice, UGB advocates can argue that compactness increases the value of the housing-neighborhood package by promoting more "real neighborhoods" along the neotraditional model. Those who argue for faster expansion counter that a tight UGB limits consumer choice by effectively blocking large lot subdivisions.

Poorer residents may benefit from bounded growth in two other ways. The housing requirements of Oregon's land use planning system have kept rental housing very affordable. The tilt toward rental construction meets the needs of many small households and the large supply of new apartments also keeps rents relatively low. At the end of 1999, the average rent for a one-bedroom apartment in the Portland market was 87 percent of the U.S. average. Average apartment rents increased only 33 percent during the 1990s; adjusted for inflation, the increase was only 5 percent.[40]

Compact development supports the viability of older industrial and warehouse districts by reducing the options for relocation. For the 1990s, Metro reported that 37 percent of new jobs were located on infill and redevelopment sites. A result is amelioration of the jobs-housing mismatch that plagues so many cities. It also helps to preserve at least a bit of the edgy, gritty, funky, and cheap space that is so important for economic and cultural innovation.

If the social impacts of compact urban form are debatable, there is little argument that it benefits the undeveloped landscape and natural systems. Most of the 13,000 acres of farmland within the Growth Boundary are destined for development, as berry fields and vegetable farms along the Columbia River flood plain grow bumper crops of tilt-up flex buildings and wheat fields turn into subdivisions. But current land use plans, with a boost from the Endangered Species Act, protect nature in the city—the open spaces of steep slopes, willow-choked stream margins, and the interlinked ecosystem of streams and wetlands. The interest of environmental advocates in Portland growth management links closely to the same sense of physical limits that influenced the origins of LCDC, for relatively little urbanizable land remains between the suburban frontier and the edges of the Northwest forest. Environmental groups have therefore been strong supporters of a compact metropolis with its bias toward urban social and cultural values.

A representative issue was the West Side Bypass, briefly noted in the previous section. The Bypass was a one-sixth circumferential highway proposed to meet lateral transportation needs in fast growing Washington County. The county's electronics industry strongly favored the bypass, as did state transportation officials. Expected opposition came from environmentalists unhappy with any highway system expansion as promoting wasteful auto-centered living. Other opponents worried specifically that the proposed route, which looped through rural land outside the UGB, would inevitably encourage sprawl.

A well-established advocate for strong land use planning, 1000 Friends of Oregon, took the lead in blending the environmental and planning critiques. It used the bypass as the case study for the nationally funded 1996 LUTRAQ study (Making the Land Use, Transportation, Air Quality Connection). LUTRAQ extended costs-of-sprawl analysis of alternative urban form to impacts on air quality and automobile use—with results favoring compact transit-oriented development. Over a period of several years, the combination of grassroots and expert opposition shifted the terms of the transportation planning debate and branded the freeway, in the words of Keith Bartholomew of 1000 Friends, as "nothing more than a $300+ million boondoggle, community wrecker, and urban growth boundary buster." [41] Heightened political costs made the bypass unpalatable to both county and state elected officials, and the Oregon Department of Transportation killed the idea in September 1995.

By the 1990s, the majority of *involved* citizens in both Portland and suburbs shared a basic vision of a metropolis that above all else is "Not-Los Angeles" and "Not-Seattle" (even if their images of these places may be unrealistic caricatures). They agree that the best way to avoid the gridlock and endless subdivisions that presumably characterize their west coast neighbors is to support relatively compact land development within the constraints of the Urban Growth Boundary. In 1994, Metro received 17,000 responses to a mail-in questionnaire about regional planning issues. Half the responses included additional write-in comments. The feedback strongly favored higher densities, smaller lots, and transit-oriented development.

The consensus is nourished by an array of "good planning" and

| Portland | 513,325 | Tualatin | 22,535 |
|---|---|---|---|
| Vancouver | 137,500 | Milwaukie | 20,250 |
| Gresham | 86,430 | Newberg | 18,275 |
| Hillsboro | 72,630 | Forest Grove | 17,130 |
| Beaverton | 70,230 | Troutdale | 14,300 |
| Tigard | 38,835 | Wilsonville | 13,615 |
| Lake Oswego | 34,305 | Canby | 13,170 |
| McMinnville | 25,250 | Gladstone | 12,020 |
| Oregon City | 24,940 | Camas | 11,350 |
| West Linn | 23,380 | Sherwood | 10,815 |

environmental organizations that benefit from the high level of public awareness and approach growth management with a regional perspective. Supplementing locally oriented neighborhood and watershed groups are the Audubon Society, 1000 Friends of Oregon, Livable Oregon, STOP (Sensible Transportation Options for People), the Coalition for a Livable Future, and sometimes the Metropolitan Home Builders Association. In the Portland style, these are pressure groups that speak to metropolitan concerns and utilize rational analysis and education to mobilize citizens around regulatory alternatives to metropolitan sprawl.

Nevertheless, there is substantial dissent in suburban communities (see Table 5 for suburban populations). Beaverton and Gresham may have signed on to the 2040 agenda, but several exclusively middle class suburbs south and southwest of the city have no desire to be "cured" of large lot single family development. Like their counterparts around the country, many residents in Milwaukie (population 20,000), West Linn (23,000), and Tigard (39,000) fear both the local environmental costs and the implied social diversification of compact growth. Milwaukie voters recalled several City Council members because of their support of light rail and 2040 housing targets. "Metro planners moan about the suburbs as if they were a disease," complained West Linn City Council member John Jackley in 1996, "and do their best to plan us out of existence with their 'urban village' concepts, functional plans and density dictates." The mayor of Tigard objected that the 2040 plan precludes large lot, up-scale developments and other "lifestyle opportunities that Tigard has always had the opportunity to provide." [42]

The May 2000 primary election for local offices was a good gauge of public attitudes. Candidates who advocate active implementation of the 2040 goals gained decisive support within the city. In Washington County, in contrast, an avowed "growth manager" candidate for Metro Councilor eked out a narrow win over a "let-the-suburbs-be-suburbs" candidate.

In the 1990s, metropolitan political battles generally circled around the policy margins. The Metropolitan Home Builders Association complained about the details of growth management regulations, not the concept. In turn, the consensus has been broad enough to attract the support of key state leaders such as Governor John Kitzhaber. Nevertheless, the people of Oregon delivered a shock to growth management in November 2000. Fifty-four percent voted to approve Measure 7, a state constitutional amendment that requires state and local governments to compensate land owners if public regulations reduce the value of their property. The measure exempts ordinances to abate nuisances and those required by the federal government, but it promises to add enormous costs to most environmental and land use regulations. The full meaning of the measure will not be known until it has been thoroughly litigated by its opponents and advocates, but it has the potential to undermine many of the protections for landscape and cityscape that have made Oregon special.

Lewis Mumford spoke to the Portland City Club on July 15, 1938 about "Rebuilding Our Cities." Mumford's landmark book, *The Culture of Cities*, was hot off the press, and his year included an appearance on the cover of *Time*. He was in Portland at the invitation of the Northwest Regional Council, a private organization that the Rockefeller Foundation had funded to advocate for regional planning and economic development. Its board of academics and New Dealers wanted him to "observe and critically appraise the growth and development of the region."

In the course of his luncheon address, Mumford issued a ringing challenge that Portlanders still invoke (much as they invoke Tom McCall's 1973 speech):

Rebuilding our cities will be one of the major tasks of the next generation. While people are grasping for personal gain, the necessary cooperative spirit for this task cannot develop.... I've seen a lot of fine country, but I've seen nothing more tempting as a home for man as I've viewed in this wonderful Oregon country during the last three days from the McKenzie River to Portland. And the view I had from the Columbia River Highway has knocked me flat. It is one of the greatest in the world. You have here the basis for civilization on its highest scale, and I am going to ask you a question which you may not like. Are you good enough to have this country in your possession? Have you got enough intelligence, imagination and cooperation among you to make the best use of these opportunities? ... In providing for such developments [hydroelectric power] you have an opportunity here to do a job of city planning like nowhere else in the world. Oregon is one of the last places in this country where natural resources are still largely intact. Are you intelligent enough to use them wisely? [43]

Behind the exhortation was Mumford's preference for a specific sort of landscape. He wanted to persuade Portlanders to follow the precepts of the Regional Planning Association of America by dispersing growth within a network of moderate sized communities that revolved around the city while preventing the excessive growth of the city itself. He was worried that power from Bonneville might industrialize the Columbia River Gorge itself or turn Portland into another Pittsburgh. His solution was regional planning, urban containment, and a balance of jobs and housing in smaller satellite cities.

Portlanders today find the vision inspiring and Mumford himself a touchstone, cited by planning and environmental advocates such as Mike Houck of the Audubon Society and Ethan Seltzer of Portland State University. However, the city and region are just beginning to construct institutional links between the tri-county core and the larger region. The Bureau of the Census now finds that economic interaction links together two million people in eight counties as a Portland-Salem CMSA, but people on the ground find that a very "soft" affiliation. Despite the statistics on commuting between the metropolitan periphery and the core counties, many members of outlying communities are reluctant recruits. Benign as Portland may be in comparison to Chicago or Philadelphia, it is an off-putting or even fearful place to many in its region—a dangerous big city that seduces the young and impressionable and expresses the cultural difference between foothills and progressive core. Portland novelist Katherine Dunn remembers its allure from the early 1960s:

When I was a bookish, goggle-eyed teen in a small hamlet twenty miles up the road, Portland was the town I ran away to, a mecca of sinister excitements. Borrowing my dad's car keys on a Saturday night could take me on a cruise of life's mysteries. With my heart thumping like a burglar's, I'd plunge in, greedy to see for myself all the terrifying things that to a country kid spelled c-i-t-y: crime, grime, danger and art, the glories of the underworld. . . . Portland gave me what I was looking for. . . . I flattened my nose on the windows of tattoo shops and pawnbrokers. . . . Jazz riffs seeping out of a basement bistro and the click of balls from the open door of a pool hall were theme music for dark adventure.[44]

This social distance suggests that outlying counties may identify more easily with larger topographical regions that overlap the
economically based CMSA than with Portland itself. Many in Columbia County think they have more in common with downriver towns
such as Longview and Cathlamet in Washington and Astoria in Oregon. Yamhill County raised shouts of dismay when the census added
it to metropolitan Portland in the 1980s and just as easily affili-
ates with Salem and its surrounding farm communities of the mid-
Willamette Valley. Clark County, Washington depends on Portland
jobs but looks to Washington legislators and officials in Olympia
when it faces its own problems of growth.

Clark County is actually Portland's little planning secret. In recent
years, it has been the fastest growing segment of the metropolitan
area. Untrammeled by Oregon's strict land use system, Clark County
has been a safety valve that offers an easy location for residents and
builders who like the low density suburban model. Growth has just
begun to slow after a decade of boom times and Washington growth
management regulations are just being felt.

Indeed, Clark County development patterns will be increasingly
constrained by Washington's Growth Management Act. Passed in
1990 and amended in 1991, the Act is mandatory for the state's large
and fast growing counties. As in the Oregon system, Clark County
is required to prepare a plan that responds to statewide goals, including creation of an urban services boundary, although the state
has limited power to alter the content of local plans. As the Washington state system is still being fully implemented, the effects are
unpredictable. Substantial political conflicts over development and
infrastructure within Clark County divide the older city of Vancouver,
rapidly suburbanizing areas, and rural districts. Regulations that
favor compact development patterns have the possibility of diverting growth pressure to Oregon and complicating the careful tradeoffs of the 2040 Plan.

Looking south rather than north, Portlanders see the hundred-mile expanse of the Willamette Valley: 4000 square miles of valley floor and 8000 square miles of hills and mountainsides. Written Walamut, Wallament, and Walla Matte by early travelers, the river got its modern spelling from Lt. Charles Wilkes in 1841, just as American settlers began to stream in over the Oregon Trail. The valley has been functionally linked to Portland since the 1850s, first by steamboats and then by railroads and roads that clung to the base of the hills for good drainage, the predecessors of routes like Oregon 99W and Oregon 213.

Unified action in the valley has focused on the river itself. At the start of the twentieth century, dozens of canneries, creameries, woolen mills, and pulp mills poured organic waste into the river and its tributaries. Towns dumped untreated sewage into the flow. A stiff antipollution law of 1919 went unenforced, leaving the lower river and Portland harbor "grossly polluted."

When the Oregon Planning Board reviewed the status of the Valley in 1937, it found an "economically underdeveloped region." [45] The Valley's still sparse population did not make full use of its soils and resources. Only one-third of its farms had electricity. Erosion and pollution were undermining basic industries. Here as on the Columbia, the solution was dam building. The Planning Board endorsed the Corps of Engineers "Coordinated Water Plan" for seven major storage reservoirs on the upper tributaries. The dams would encourage agriculture by reducing floods; they would dilute pollution and furnish hydropower for economic development. In fact, the dams and their power helped Willamette Valley population double from the start of World War II to 1970. Further steps to clean up the river came in the 1960s and 1970s (as noted in Chapter 1).

It has been more difficult to find political and social linkages between Portland and the valley. The passage of land use legislation in 1973 involved a city-country coalition, but the goal for valley farmers was to keep Portland at bay. The governor in 1996 created a Willamette Valley Livability Forum to get the public and private sectors thinking about common issues. With no regulatory powers and a soft mandate to "create and promote a shared vision for enhancing the livability of the Willamette Valley," it has a predictably low profile.[46] A 1999 report, *Choices for the Future: The Willamette Valley*, was modeled on the Lawrence Halprin report of 1972 but had far less impact. Local markets and regional governmental organizations divide the valley into east-west segments centered on Eugene, Corvallis-Albany, Salem, and Portland.

In fact, this separation between Portland and the agricultural valley is as old as American settlement, which set up a cultural tension that can still be glimpsed behind Oregon policy debates. New England and New York merchants and entrepreneurs dominated the early trading towns and imported a veneer of Congregational and Presbyterian propriety. Farm families from Missouri, Illinois, Tennessee, and other central Mississippi Valley states simultaneously brought frontier self-sufficiency to the prairies and foothills. Their interests were mutual but distinct. Cities needed farmers as customers and sources of exports; farmers needed townspeople to access distant markets but deeply resented the profits that Portland businesses took off the top. Farmers named their counties for southerners: Virginia's George Washington, Missouri's Lewis Linn and Thomas H. Benton, Tennessee's James Polk, South Carolina's Francis Marion. Towns borrowed names from the Northeast —Albany, Dayton, Monmouth, Salem, Lowell, Springfield—or invoked the virtues of Amity, Independence, Sublimity. Portland's name came with the flip of a coin from Portland, Maine over Boston, Massachusetts.

It has been equally hard to create common goals for metropolitan Portland and the old farm-forest-fishing communities of the lower Columbia where boom times ended in the 1920s. The huge container ships, log ships, and ungainly Japanese auto carriers that wallow over the bar at the mouth of the Columbia and pound upriver to Longview, Portland, and Vancouver leave only lapping wakes at Astoria,

Oregon and Cathlamet, Washington. The future of the lower Columbia looks like tourism and small scale ecologically sensitive industry in the shadow of the metropolis.

There *are* efforts to create new regional connections. Ecotrust, a Portland based organization devoted to sustainable development, works on community based projects around the mouth of the river. The governors of Oregon and Washington in October 1999 announced a Lower Columbia Management Plan for the tidal river—146 miles from Bonneville Dam to the Pacific. Environmental groups, local governments, and industrial associations have signed on to a program of wetland restoration, shoreline protection, and pollution reduction for the river and 4300 square miles of adjacent upcountry. It helps that both governors are Democrats, that the plan is voluntary, and that the Endangered Species Act looms in the background. Whether the efforts help residents think of a lower Columbia region remains to be seen.

A stronger institution that formally links Portland and its hinterland is the Columbia River Gorge National Scenic Area, which attempts to blend metropolitan and rural interests in a single management process. The gorge itself is a seventy-five-mile notch through the mountains and lava flows of the Cascade mountain range. From The Dalles to the eastern outskirts of Portland, well within the metropolitan area boundaries, the Columbia has carved a passage between the northern flanks of Mount Hood in Oregon and the southern flank of Mount Adams in Washington. The river has worn its passageway through successive uplifts and outflows of lava over millions of years. Towering floods of glacial meltwater repeatedly crashed through the gorge between 16,000 and 12,800 years ago to shape its present form.

As the only passage near sea level through the Cascades and Sierra Nevada from the United States-Canada border to southern California, the gorge has been a vital transportation artery for native peoples, fur traders, steamboaters, railroads, barge tows, truckers, and automobiles. It is an historic resource producing region and is home to roughly 60,000 people in parts of Oregon and Washington, a mix of old Finnish and Scandinavian settler families, third generation Japanese Americans, Mexican orchard workers, and windsurfers. It is not a pristine environment. Over nearly two centuries American traders and settlers have drastically altered its natural environment by logging, fishing, and agriculture. Americans have impounded the river with dams at Bonneville and The Dalles, carved its shores for roads and railroads, and nearly eliminated its salmon runs. No natural resource exists in anything like its form at the time of Lewis and Clark. Nevertheless, the gorge remains a visually stunning landscape, as Lewis Mumford noted, with steep green mountains rising 4000 feet from the river and dozens of waterfalls plunging off its high plateaus and slopes.

Portlanders began to savor the scenery of the Columbia Gorge in the later nineteenth century with steamboat tours and camping expeditions. "Here wonder, curiosity, and admiration combine to arouse sentiments of awe and delight," wrote historian Frances Fuller Victor in 1891.[47] Steamboats gave way to automobile tourism with the completion of the Columbia River Highway from Portland to The Dalles in the 1910s. Sections remain in use as scenic byway or hike-bike trail within sight of the streaming traffic on I-84.

Federal legislation in 1986 to create a National Scenic Area reflected the power of Portlanders to shape a regional agenda around the goal of scenic protection. Indeed, the legislation climaxed a steady expansion of Portland's use of the gorge as a recreation zone through the twentieth century. The Scenic Area Act, however, built in tension by adding the second goal of economic development to the first goal of resource preservation. Senator Mark Hatfield reflected this understanding of the Scenic Area when he told a gorge audience that the legislation "was never intended to dry up those communities in the gorge or to be a blow to the future of those communities."[48] In specific, the legislative goals are to "(1) protect and

Columbia River Highway (Oregon Historical Society Neg. 52910). Dedicated in 1915, the Columbia River Highway was designed for both commerce and pleasure. Engineer Sam Lancaster adapted the highway to the landscape and opened the Columbia River Gorge to autoists from Portland.

provide for the enhancement of the scenic, cultural, recreational and natural resources of the Columbia River Gorge, and (2) protect and support the economy of the Gorge by encouraging growth to occur in existing urban areas and by allowing future economic development in a manner that is consistent with paragraph 1."

In effect, the act requires the Forest Service and a new bi-state Columbia River Gorge Commission, the specified management agencies, to preserve and create jobs for country people while managing scenery for city people. The tool is a land use management plan on the Oregon model, not a particularly popular choice among property rights fundamentalists on the Washington side. A homemade billboard outside Lyle, Washington depicted the Congressional proponents of the Scenic Area as horses' asses. The act divides the gorge into Special Management Areas (115,000 acres of largely federal land where little development is expected, with the Forest Service as the lead agency); General Management Areas (149,000 acres of largely private land where carefully controlled development is expected and a bi-state commission is the lead agency); and thirteen urban areas (28,500 acres that are exempt from the act and remain under local planning control). The legislation makes the gorge counties partners in implementing legislation that many residents opposed (the Scenic Area embraces parts of Clark and Multnomah Counties, where politics favors the legislation, as well as parts of four other nonmetropolitan counties where opposition was and continues to be much stronger). It also gives the four federally recognized Columbia River Indian tribes an explicit role in defining and identifying cultural resources.

The model for the Scenic Area is the European idea of "greenline parks." The term comes from the idea of drawing a "green" line on a map to define a district of high scenic or cultural value and devising special land regulations to sustain its character over time. The ap-

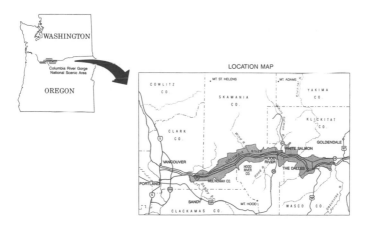

Columbia River Gorge National Scenic Area (U.S.D.A. Forest Service). The Columbia River Gorge National Scenic Area, established by Congress in 1986, begins precisely at an eastern edge of the Urban Growth Boundary, marked by the Sandy River. The Scenic Area represents Portland's interest in maintaining the Gorge as an easily accessible recreation zone.

proach is meant for working or living landscapes, not wilderness. Inside the green line, special controls can preserve natural resources, social institutions, and historic landscapes while allowing local residents to continue their previous livelihoods from land-based industries. Other examples in the United States include New York's Adirondack Park and the New Jersey Pinelands. National Parks in the United Kingdom are also specially regulated landscapes rather than public reserves in the American style.

As a greenline experiment, the Scenic Area is a multiple balancing act. As an effort to plan for environmentally sensitive economic development, it faces the challenge of reconciling sometimes competing activities within the same limited space. Protection of natural areas competes with resource production; both may conflict with new industries such as tourism. Closely related is the need to mediate between differing and sometimes clashing community cultures and worldviews that belong to an "old west" of loggers and ranchers and a "new west" of bureaucrats and Internet entrepreneurs. The intent of the Scenic Area and related programs is to plan and manage the changes that usually come piecemeal and sometimes overwhelmingly to resource regions. Substantive goals try to balance the forces of change against the claims of existing social and economic systems. Implementation requires ranchers, loggers, and other "old westerners" who pride themselves on bluntness to learn the customs of committee work and bureaucracies. It likewise expects the sophisticated city based interest groups that generated the legislation to accept rural communities as partners and agents of change.

Hopeful as we may be about structuring regional institutions, it may well be that Portland is most closely linked to its ecoregion when its landscape is obscured by cloud. In late autumn and winter, banks of morning fog will roll from the mouth of the Columbia Gorge to blanket the city. Mist will rise from the Willamette and wreath the west hills with trailing clouds that reach westward toward the ocean-seeking streams and bays. Historians Tom Vaughan and Terry O'Donnell have found Portland's character shaped by "soft rains and muffling fogs, something soothing and soporific that slows men down." [49] Some days the fog thins by midday as the sun warms the damp marine air that has drifted in from the Pacific. On other days—book-reading days—the city is never unwrapped.

A generation ago, Glen Coffield saw the lifting mist in "Crossing Hawthorne Bridge."

> One morning while crossing Hawthorne bridge,
> The seagulls were soaring in magnificent arcs,
> And a slight trace of fog was banked against
> The houses on the opposite cliffs. Despite
>
> A chill, the sun was breaking through here
> And there, and it was a fine morning. . . .[50]

More recent is Tim Barnes's "Winter Fog Along the Willamette."

> 1
> The hills across the river
> turn slowly to mist
> this afternoon, all
> the way to the coast,
> trees fade from
> their forests, farms
> leave their chickens
> and goats, housewives
> look out windows into a vanished
> yard. Toddlers drift
> from their trikes.

The crow and his cry
are lost where rivers
wave to their beds.
A sigh that is almost
a shudder
breaks from the bull
in the field as he chews
the thoughtful grass
down to simply nothing.


2

It is similar to snow,
to TV static, an
interference of air.
Your best friends
evaporate in the distance,
the way roads blow
away into winter.
No knobs or wheels
can recall them.


There is nothing to fix,
now, nothing to focus.
Your hands, your eyes,
no longer hold
what you wish,
which, at this moment
is only your body—
that it might remain with you
in any weather on earth.[51]

Lewis and Clark Exposition by day (Oregon Historical Society Neg. 28137). The temporary frame and plaster buildings of the Lewis and Clark Exposition transformed vacant land and an intermittent lake into "a diamond set on a coronet of emerald"in the summer of 1905.

## ON THE RIM OF THE PACIFIC

One of Portland's grandest parades started at the corner of Sixth and Montgomery Streets at 10 A.M. on June 1, 1905. Mounted police led off, followed by marching bands, 2000 National Guardsmen, and more police to bring up the rear. As the marchers trooped up Sixth, their ranks opened in front of the elegant Portland Hotel to make way for the carriage of Vice President Charles Fairbanks. Their destination was Northwest Portland and the inaugural ceremony for the Lewis and Clark Centennial Exposition, where the opening day crowd of 40,000 could listen to a dozen long speeches about the importance of Portland and its world's fair.

Visitors who drifted away from the oratory discovered 400 acres of fairgrounds planned by Frederick Law Olmsted, Jr. to encircle the shallow waters of Guild's Lake. The formal layout of lath and plaster buildings imitated the Chicago fair of 1893. Exhibition buildings overlooked the lake from a low bluff. A wide staircase led downslope to "The Trail," the amusement arcade where the wonders of the world were available for a dime or quarter. A Bridge of Nations connected the mainland to the U.S. government buildings showcasing federal resource agencies. The whitewashed stucco of the buildings gleamed against the West Hills like "diamonds set in a coronet of emeralds."

From June 1 through October 15, nearly 1.6 million people paid for admission to the first world's fair on the Pacific coast of North America. Four hundred thousand of them were from beyond the Pacific Northwest. They could attend highminded conferences on education, civic affairs, and the future of the United States in the Orient or participate in national conventions of librarians, social workers, physicians, and railroad conductors. They could inspect the exhibits of sixteen states and twenty-one foreign nations. They could fritter their money on "The Streets of Cairo" and the "Carnival of Venice."

The city's business leaders gave wholehearted support to planning and promoting the exposition, for its purpose was a bigger and better Portland. It was an age when every ambitious city aspired to put on a national or international fair. The list already included Philadelphia, Atlanta, Nashville, Chicago, Omaha, Buffalo, and St. Louis; soon after the Portland fair would come events in Norfolk, Seattle, San Diego, and San Francisco. The fair was to show outside investors that Portland was a mature and "finished" city rather than a frontier town. It was also intended to give Portland an edge over upstart Seattle and confirm its role as a commercial center for the Pacific. The official title of the event was the "Lewis and Clark Centennial and American Pacific Exposition and Oriental Fair." The motto over the entrance was "Westward the Course of Empire Takes Its Way." The biggest foreign exhibit came from Japan. Jefferson Myers, chair of the committee overseeing the state's involvement, went straight to the point in testimony to Congress: "If all the wheat raised west of the Mississippi River were ground into flour for the China trade, the consumption per Chinaman would not exceed one pancake per month." A visiting journalist agreed that "the whole fair is a success-ful effort to express . . . the natural richness of the country and its relative nearness to Asia." [52]

Portland's interest in the Pacific trade was shared by all the cities of the coast. Business people anticipated an explosion of trade when the Panama Canal tied the Pacific and Atlantic worlds. Journalists caught Panama Canal fever and penned stories about "The Coming Supremacy of the Pacific." In California, historian and history pub-lisher Hubert Howe Bancroft had recently combined a boosterish inventory of western resources with the ancient trope of the west-ward course of empire in *The New Pacific*. The twentieth century, he proclaimed, would be the century of the *new* Pacific, with North Americans shouldering aside tired Europeans and the wealth of the Pacific surpassing that of the Atlantic. The vision was one of classic liberalism, with free trade in goods and ideas lifting the strongest individuals and nations to success.

The far west facing the far east, with the ocean between, have lain hitherto at the back door of both Europe and America. Now by magic strides the antipo-dal No-man's-land is coming to the front to claim a proper share in the world's doings. . . .

We have no longer a virgin continent to develop; pioneer work in the United States is done, and now we must take a plunge into the sea. Here we find an area, an amphitheatre of water, upon and around which American enterprise and industry, great as it is and greatly to be increased, will find occupation for the full term of the twentieth century, and for many centuries thereafter. The Pacific, its shores and islands, must now take the place of the great west, its plains and mountains, as an outlet for pent-up industry. Here on this ocean all the world will meet, and on equal footing, Americans and Europeans, Asiatics and Afri-cans, white, yellow, and black, looters and looted, the strongest and cunningest to carry off the spoils.[53]

Nearly a century after the Exposition, Portland is certainly a participant in a Pacific economic system that may surpass even Bancroft's expectations.

In its maritime trade Portland is somewhat like baseball's old Washington Senators. It plays in the major leagues of Pacific ports, but finds itself relegated to the bottom of the standings, trailing Long Beach, Los Angeles, Oakland, Seattle, and Vancouver. Portland has one of the highest import-export tonnages among west coast ports because of bulk exports of lumber, grain, and minerals and imports of steel and automobiles (it is one of the top five auto ports in the United States). But it falls behind its competitors in the value of its cargos, serving only 2–3 percent of west coast container trade (see Chapter 1).

It was high tech manufacturing that pushed Portland forward as an international trader in the 1990s and into the new century. The annual value of high tech exports doubled from 1994 to 1997 (at $3.2 billion). Much of the enormously high value/low weight output of the Silicon Suburbs goes by air to foreign markets, especially in Asia; air cargo shipments increased from 45,000 tons in 1980 to 136,000 in 1990 and 273,000 in 1999.[54] The Portland-Vancouver PMSA in 1997 ranked twentieth among metropolitan areas in manufacturing employment and tenth in the value of exports, outselling larger regions such as Boston and Philadelphia. In the 1980s Oregon's raw material exports (wood, wheat, and other farm products) were worth nearly twice as much as its exports of manufactured goods. By the later 1990s, the situation was reversed with electronics, business machinery, computers, and transportation equipment the leading sectors.[55]

These are the sort of economic data that feed talk of an emerging binational economic region of "Cascadia." Proponents of a business-based Cascadia argue that residents of the urbanized Vancouver-Eugene corridor share both values and economic interests. The people of this I-5 Main Street agree, says Alan Artibise, in their love of the outdoors, sense of isolation from Ottawa or Washington, D.C., orientation to Asian markets, openness to Asian immigrants, and involvement in the rise of the information economy. Boosters see an integrated economic region that pools the capacity of Portland, Seattle, Vancouver, and their hinterlands into a city region with the clout to compete with Los Angeles, Sydney, Osaka-Kobe, Seoul, and Shanghai. Depiction of such a Cascadia draws on the popular and plausible idea that "city-states" rather than nations are the real engines of contemporary economies. Originating with Jane Jacobs in the 1980s, the idea is now common wisdom in both the United States and Europe (where it makes sense in the context of the European Union). The idea of a Triple Entente among Vancouver, Seattle, and Portland is also an extrapolation of the New Northwest economy. In the most expansive view, this metropolitan corridor carries along as many as five states (Oregon, Washington, Idaho, Montana, Alaska), two provinces (British Columbia, Alberta), and the Yukon territory.

To date, however, economic Cascadia is a set of ideas and committees rather than a natural economic unit. National pride and identity still override efforts to define common agendas for the organization of economic *production*. NAFTA has loosened trade, but immigration and capital investment still take place within national borders. It makes a difference whether a Korean electronics firm decides to invest its $2 billion in Oregon or British Columbia. It makes a difference whether someone from Hong Kong decides to move to Vancouver or Seattle. The government of British Columbia blocked the implementation of a Cascadia Corridor Commission (authorized by both national governments) because of fears of subordination to Seattle. Canadian concerns have been heightened by the effects of NAFTA on Canadian branch plant manufacturing. The idea of a multinational Cascadian region has been most visible in advertisements for a "two-nation vacation" and cell phone ads offering service throughout "Portlecouver" and "Vanseacoma."

When we take a clearer look at Main Street Cascadia, we also find that the three cities are too distant from each other for effective everyday interaction (ask any Portland basketball fan her opinion of having the Trail Blazers managed from Seattle). Each metropolis is large enough to support a full range of consumer and producer services (NBA teams, research hospitals, advertising firms). Except for matters of taste, a Portlander need not go to Vancouver to seek out a sophisticated architectural firm, and a Vancouverite need not go to Seattle for transpacific container service or air connections. In short, the cities may be too similar to form a complementary whole on the analogy of the San Francisco Bay area, where high finance San Francisco, high tech San Jose, thoughtful Berkeley, and brawny Oakland work as a metropolitan team.

A realistic expectation for Main Street Cascadia may be less a merger of well-matched parts than a federation of otherwise similar city-states—a sort of Hanseatic League for the twenty-first century. The northwest cities originated, grew, and have continued to prosper as east-west gateways, not north-south connectors. Each is fundamentally a gateway to the Pacific and Asia for continental economies and a service center for interior hinterlands. British Columbia does a *smaller* proportion of its trade with the United States than does the rest of Canada.

Another argument against the likelihood of a fully realized Cascadian economy is the looming presence of California, that vortex of economic power and engine of demographic and cultural change with the capacity to overwhelm smaller neighbors. There are ten of them—Californians—for every one of us Oregonians; there are ten of them—residents of greater Los Angeles—for every person in greater Portland. Northward connections have been important for the northwestern United States, but southward ones even more so. In Oregon we *know* that we're a stubby little tail wagged by the very large California dog. Since 1849 California has been the market, population pool, corporation headquarters, and consumption arena that pulls Oregon, Idaho, and Washington southward from Canada and Cascadia. Even Microsoft had to wait for California entrepreneurs to create the PC revolution. The regional agricultural center of Yakima, Washington has more in common with Bakersfield, California than with Kamloops, British Columbia. As historian John Findlay points out, the northwestern United States has often forged its regional identity as a contrast to California. The Golden State is the missing guest in discussions of Cascadia, waiting to take over the debate just as the statue of the Commandatore takes over the final act of *Don Giovanni*.

A very different understanding of Portland as part of a Pacific Rim region has alternative roots in an environmentalist rethinking of western America. In the mid-1970s, Ernest Callenbach's utopian novel *Ecotopia* was a surprise bestseller.[56] Writing in the shadow of energy shortages, Callenbach envisioned a 1999 in which northern California, Oregon, and Washington split from the United States to follow a path of soft energy and socially inclusive development. In the style of the genre, Callenbach unfolded the traits of Ecotopia and its alternative America through the eyes of a visiting journalist exposed to a society structured around deep ecology and feminism.

A quarter century later, when the energy crisis of the 1970s is a largely forgotten inconvenience, few read *Ecotopia*. Joel Garreau claimed the term but not the social program as the name for one of his *Nine Nations of North America* in 1981. Portlanders like to recycle, and City Council has required Starbucks and McDonalds to substitute paper cups and boxes for styrofoam. But community organizing efforts that once focused on local self-sufficiency have given way to community development corporations that try to jump-start the private housing market. The name "ecotopia" survived the 1970s in Portland only in ironic use and has now vanished from the phone book.

The heir of the Ecotopian ideal is not local policies or organizations but a vision of "Cascadia" as the setting for environmentally light or sensitive development. The most eloquent statement has been Seattle University professor David McCloskey's map of a "great green land on the northeast Pacific Rim." McCloskey's Cascadia is an effort to forge a new awareness of human relationships with the regional landscape. But it also harkens back to the Old West economy and the age of mobility in which resources trumped political borders. McCloskey's evocative map (drawn in 1988) pictures the northwest coast as a great exotic leaf, veined with delicate networks of streams and rivers from Cape Mendocino to Yakutut Bay. Provinces, states, and nations disappear under the imperative of the hydrologic cycle that endlessly links Pacific Slope and Pacific Ocean, the same cycle that created and sustained forests and fish runs. Other activist depictions of an ecological Cascadia, such as Ecotrust's book on *The Rain Forests of Home* and maps of the coastal temperate rain forest, emphasize the north-south extensions of mountains and troughs that link the landscape and bioscape (and that carried early settlers and workers easily north and south).[57]

All this inspiring rhetoric being noted, we find ourselves back at the bureaucratic realization that environments at the beginning of the twenty-first century are protected through laws, regulations, and plans. The powerful Columbia River was confined by dams in the last gasp of the Old West economy. Now it is managed by a Northwest Power Planning Council, a Bonneville Power Administration, a Columbia River Gorge National Scenic Area, a Columbia River Inter-Tribal Fish Commission, and dozens of other complex organizations that try to balance the conflicting demands of industries, nations, communities, and peoples. Systematic care for the Great Raincoast of North America, to use Richard Maxwell Brown's term, will require similar institution building.

Portland, meanwhile, in its typical fashion, marks its old and new Pacific connections with symbolic ties and with landscapes. With a handful of exceptions, the central city and suburbs have chosen sis-

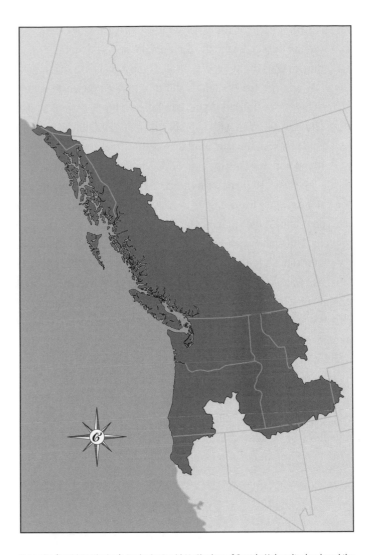

Cascadia (David McCloskey). Ecologist David McCloskey of Seattle University developed the idea of the natural region of Cascadia in the 1980s. In a series of maps he has depicted the network of rivers that tie Cascadia to the sea, defined the subregions of Cascadia, and demonstrated the way the natural region crosses and disdains state and national boundaries.

ter cities from Pacific nations as far flung as Nicaragua, Australia, and Siberian Russia. Sister city Sapporo, Japan has donated a wind sculpture for Waterfront Park. Suzhou, China has given a seventeen-ton rock in return for Portland's gift of a rose garden. The water-shaped limestone boulder from Lake Tai, now firmly settled across from City Hall, is laden with symbolic meaning in Chinese culture. In the old skid road district (and across the street from a new Port of Portland building), a city block was shaped into a Chinese garden in the classical Suzhou tradition. Suzhou's garden bureau was the chief designer for the meticulously arranged buildings, plantings, pool, and bridges that recreate the style of that city's sixty-nine gardens. The Chinese Garden, opened in September 2000, complements Portland's Japanese Garden. Now in its fourth decade, the Japanese Garden is a point of attachment for Japanese visitors and a center of activities for various Japanese American organizations. It shares Washington Park, west of downtown, with other landscapes of enjoyment and commemoration—rose garden, arboretum, Vietnam veterans' memorial, planned holocaust memorial.

With their miniaturized worlds of mountains and lakes, the Chinese and Japanese gardens bring us full circle to the Forecourt Fountain. Here too, in a very different idiom, are Portland's natural surroundings encapsulated. Even at its most cosmopolitan, Portland is a city that foregrounds a sense of its place in the landscape.

# Conclusion
# Civic Opportunity

Seattle? Sure. But Indianapolis? Kansas City? Columbus?

Portland on paper has an interesting set of peer cities. Take the nation's second level metropolitan areas with populations of 1 to 3 million—pick a score of social and economic indicators such as percentage foreign-born, median educational attainment, industrial distribution of workers, and the like—and find the places whose socioeconomic profile resembles Portland.

Despite obvious differences in style and tone, Seattle is a close match. Less expected as statistical siblings are cities along the American main street—the old National Road, U.S. 40, I-70. Start on East Broad Street in Columbus and end on West Colfax Street in Denver. Along the way are Indianapolis and Kansas City. Another city with a Portland feel is Cincinnati, a conservative town of river, hills, and neighborhoods. The peripatetic Generation X spokesman of *Monk* magazine recently described Portland's "coastal intelligence matched with a Midwestern scale and pace."[1] There *is* a certain middle westernness to Portland in its moderate scale, slow tempo, informality, and self-satisfaction.

Such similarities are reminders of the power of history. Apart from the New Englanders in the towns, most of the early settlers of the Willamette Valley came from the Ohio and Missouri valleys,

Portland in 1889 (Oregon Historical Society Neg. 23627). Portland in 1889 was poised for economic takeoff and the explosive growth of the east side. Shown are cut-over hills behind downtown, the first streets of Portland Heights, and the original Morrison Bridge (1887) and Steel Bridge (1889).

making Oregon a far finger of the Middle West. Despite the ethnicity of South Portland, most of the city's immigrants came from the littoral of the North Sea rather than southern or eastern Europe. The similarities are also reminders that Portland grew as a particular type of city, a regional metropolis in the typology of Otis Duncan. What makes Portland different from other such places as Atlanta or Denver is not regional orientation in itself, but rather the extraordinary characteristics of its particular hinterland and history. This is precisely the insight journalist Ernie Pyle reported in 1936:

Everybody here is crazy about Portland. They rave about it. They don't talk Chamber of Commerce folders; they don't talk about their industries and their schools and their crops. They roar about what a wonderful place Portland is just to live in.

People *do* live well here. This whole Northwest country is beautiful, and the climate is pleasant, and existence is gentle.

Portland is a place, they say, where money doesn't get you anywhere so-

CONCLUSION

cially. I asked what *does* get you somewhere—what, in other words, was the standard for social admittance in Portland? They thought and they thought. They finally decided that the standard was merely an ability to contribute something—usually agreeableness and interest.

It was settled by "down Easters" who came around the Horn. They made the money and became the backbone. They're still the backbone and the pacesetters of Portland thought. But they have somehow mixed their New England soundness with a capacity for living the freer, milder Northwest way, and it makes a pretty high-class combination.[2]

Like residents of Indianapolis or Denver or the fictional Zenith of George Babbitt, Portlanders are proud of themselves. They can be formidable boosters of their home community. Ask around town and you'll learn that Portland is special for its climate ("mild," not rainy), its views of snowcapped Mount Hood, its small town ambience and "just folks" style, *and* its success at fending off many problems of urban congestion and sprawl. New Yorkers either love it because you can actually relax or hate it because there's no *edge* to anything. In health conscious Portland, Blake Nelson's exiled poet chainsmokes to keep a connection to the raspy life of lower Manhattan. But standing at the foot of Multnomah Falls, "Mark's cigarette is going out. It's too wet here."[3] In this self-satisfied picture of achievement by avoidance and healthy living, Los Angeles has long been damned. Seattle has sold its soul. Only Portland still treads the strait way of good planning.

Portlanders are pleased provincials, and Portland's conceit is the satisfaction of self-sufficiency. New York, to personify a contrast, blithely dismisses American rivals, measures itself against Paris and Tokyo, and proclaims itself the champion of the world. Portland is satisfied with its place and pace—its position in both the economic and natural landscapes and the patterns of life its landscapes support. It is a city, to quote a recent observer, whose tone is set by "people who fully occupy themselves locally."[4]

A fascinating example is the musical career of Marv and Rindy Ross. Oregon school teachers who formed a successful Portland bar and club band in the early 1980s, they scored a national recording contract as "Quarterflash" and an MTV hit in "Harden My Heart" (with Rindy playing saxophone and contributing spectacular vocals). Rather than trying to hang on in the fiercely competitive national music scene, however, they returned to regional roots, assembling local musicians into the "Trail Band" to perform Northwest music from the era of the Oregon Trail to the present. The Trail Band enlists first-line skills for a regional audience of community festivals and "cool little community theaters," to quote Marv Ross. As I was putting the final touches on this manuscript, I heard them at an upscale party marking 150 years of *The Oregonian* (another regionally entrenched institution). I challenge anyone to find a more rousing rendition of "Roll On, Columbia."

Outsiders might freely dismiss Portland's self-satisfaction as the standard wares of hot air merchants were it not shared by many well-informed observers around the nation. Portland enjoys a strong reputation in the circles of urban planning and policy as a well planned and livable metropolitan community. The city and region gained initial attention in the late 1970s and 1980s and enjoyed a surge of positive commentary in the 1990s and beyond. Inspection junkets have become a steady contributor to the Portland tourist economy. Journalists try to discover "how Portland does it," to use the question posed by Philip Langdon in 1992.[5] One civic delegation after another makes the rounds and tries the patience of local leaders in search of lessons for their own city.

Spanning city boundaries, the Portland area is a prime exhibit for innovative institutions for the management of metropolitan growth and services. In a burst of institutional creativity in the 1970s, the Oregon legislature crafted a statewide system for mandated land use planning, and the voters of the three core metropolitan counties created an elected regional government. The U.S. Department

Downtown from East Bank (photo by author). Downtown Portland from the northeast: Tom McCall Waterfront Park, extra-high towers for Portland's two major banks (now absorbed by out-of-towners), and modest high rises for the city's corporations and law firms.

of Housing and Urban Development recently credited regionwide cooperation for supporting a successful transition from traditional manufacturing to a knowledge-based economy.

It is instructive to look behind the quality of life ratings that earned Portland favorable attention in the 1970s. Arthur Louis named it the fourth best city in a *Harper's Magazine* article in 1975, while Ben-Chieh Liu put it first in a 200-factor ranking for federal agencies. Although nobody was yet using the term "social capital," that is what was being measured. Liu placed Portland first because of educational levels, library circulation, public parks, homeownership, voter turnout, newspaper readership, and similar factors.[6] Portland dropped to the middle of the pack in the 1980s, especially in *Places Rated Almanac* and *Money* magazine, which emphasized the quantity of big city amenities and economic variables during Oregon's timber recession. One of Portland's best placements in *Money* (1990) was only 38th, behind Tacoma and Richland, Washington; residents of the Northwest know why these are puzzling results. Portland has continued its mixed reviews in the business press: good for entrepreneurship, less so for income. "The work ethic is excellent," *Fortune* has said, "even though many workers need occasional sprees among the trees."[7] The city remained strong on specialized lists that focused on physical environment and civic capacity.

Portland has rich social capital and nationally admired institutions for citizen involvement and civic action because a set of challenges familiar to many U.S. cities have interacted with a distinctive political culture. Robert Kaplan writes not only that Portland pedestrians wait for green lights, but that the city "has the atmosphere of a Scandinavian country, where almost everyone shares a background and values, and trusts the centralizing and controlling force of local government to preserve these things."[8] The result—when it works—has been a rare conjunction of public and private interest. Portlanders inhabit their region very self-consciously and deliberately, even if they are not unanimous in the goals they seek.

Portland's civic activism in the 1980s and 1990s can be compared to similar eras elsewhere. One well-known example is Birmingham, England from the 1850s through the 1880s, when the business leadership espoused a "civic gospel." The civic culture drew on the social values of nonconformist religion to shape city government as an effective servant of all the people. An American journalist in 1890 rated Birmingham the best governed city in the world. An example in the United States is Chicago's "civic moment" from the 1890s to the 1920s, when business concerns and public interest converged around the physical redesign of the metropolis. Much of the private sector was self-consciously "public" in rhetoric and often in reality. Middle class women as well as men shared a vision of a reformed city that was implicitly assimilationist. The well-oiled economic machinery of the metropolis would have a place for everyone; improved housing and public services would help integrate newcomers into the social fabric (though the vision foundered on the rocks of labor-management conflict and black immigration). Portland's civic action might also be compared to the locally activated

CONCLUSION

reinvention of cities such as Glasgow or Barcelona in the late twentieth century.

The "civic moment" is fragile. The community consensus in Portland is continually under challenge—not from machine politics as in Boston or Chicago, but from the values of privatism. In the face of neoconservative national discourse that devalues the public realm, Portlanders must constantly tend and maintain their forums and institutions for civic discourse and community action. This challenge extends both to formal civic institutions and to the informal public places that nurture social capital. Moderate size has allowed Portland room for experiment, but success has meant growth and the need to acculturate newcomers into the "Portland way." I have described this Portland style in terms of civic culture. For people who enjoy French theorists, it is similar to the concept that Pierre Bourdieu dresses up in Latin as *habitus*, meaning shared predispositions and common ideas about how the world does and should work that arise out of the experience of living in particular places.

Oregon is also a place where strong individualism tempers and challenges strong communities. In many ways it has been a classically "liberal" society in which few social institutions have intervened between citizens and self-interest. Oregon has low church membership and attendance, tied with Alaska for second-to-last place behind unsanctified Nevada. Low church association and "pioneer" individualism mean low contributions to charity, with Oregon showing up two-thirds of the way down a state by state "generosity index" based on the ratio of itemized deductions to adjusted gross income on federal tax returns.[9] Ethnic groups have limited political salience or cultural power (in contrast to Boston Irish, Detroit Poles, or Chicago African Americans). Labor unions have been weak, especially as the twentieth century wore along. The mediating role that these traditional institutions play in eastern cities has to be filled by consciously created civic groups: neighborhood associations, "Friends of" groups, City Club, Association for Portland Progress.

"Fifth Avenue, Portland, Oregon, 6:30 a.m." (Gordon Gilkey, photo lithograph, 1997, Visual Chronicle of Portland). Gordon Gilkey's photo lithograph shows a high rise center that could be a model for Hugh Feriss's fantastic drawings of looming skyscrapers. What sets Portland apart from Dallas or Denver is not its high rise architecture but the liveliness of the streets below. Short blocks and street level commercial space meet the design prescriptions of urban critics Jane Jacobs and William H. Whyte.

Environmental organizations such as the Nature Conservancy and Audubon Society are especially strong. Balancing historically low levels of charitable giving, Oregon has more nonprofit organizations with federal 501(c)(3) tax status per capita than most other states.

Portland, in other words, is an "intentional metropolitan community." The term is meant to imply both vision and fragility. Intentional communities range from co-housing projects to communes, from secular utopian settlements to separatist religious enclaves. They are motivated by a dream of doing things better, and quickly collapse when visions diverge. Functioning on a much larger scale than Brook Farm or New Harmony, Portland's vision is less comprehensive, but it is still ethically based.

Portland's newspapers and its community leaders carefully mon-

CONCLUSION

itor their progress toward civic goals. We've mentioned the City Club, with its regular research reports on issues of governance, growth, and community values (meaning the regulation of prostitution, the state as a promoter of gambling addiction, and similar problems). The Club's attempt to define a "Vision for Portland's Future" in 1980 influenced thinking during the next decade. The Columbia-Willamette Futures Forum and the Civic Index project in the 1980s examined patterns of leadership, community participation, and other aspects of civic capacity. Portland Future Focus followed by defining an agenda of action issues for the 1990s. The Central City Summit in 1998–99 placed environment and education at the top of the civic to-do list.

One problem that faces "intentional" Portland, as it does many other cities, is the replacement of local business leadership by outside ownership. Outside takeover of Evans Products in the early 1980s removed a progressive civic voice. Georgia Pacific transferred its corporate headquarters to Atlanta to be closer to southern pine forests. In the second half of the 1990s, San Francisco and Minneapolis banking conglomerates absorbed the city's two biggest banks, with roots in the pioneer generation. One electric utility has been taken over by Texans and resold to Nevadans, while another has gone to Scottish capitalists. Large national corporations have engrossed other locally rooted corporations: Jantzen (sportswear), Freightliner (trucks), Hyster (heavy equipment), Fred Meyer (retailing). Will these corporate resources continue to be available for creative responses to community problems, or will involvement be confined to safe contributions to the United Way?

Like many other provincial cities, Portland has also experienced the out-migration of individual wealth. Since the days of lumber king Simon Benson and lawyer-litterateur C. E. S. Wood early in the twentieth century, many Portland "swells" have chosen to retire to California. Peculiarities of state tax policy (no sales tax in Oregon, no state income tax in Washington) have made Clark County a junior grade tax refuge and drawn a number of affluent Portlanders to new mansions overlooking the Columbia River from the north. To date the tax refugees have remained engaged with the metropolis—making up a full third of the largest contributors to the Oregon Symphony, for example—but it would be no surprise if their attention gradually drifted away.

Another worry is the problem that consensual politics leave little room for principled dissent, for they assume basic agreement on community goals. With all its virtues, the Portland style tends to muffle radically dissenting voices who are unwilling to work on the "team." Although advocates of the Portland consensus would disagree, it is possible that a pattern of cooptation stifles a serious hearing for good ideas by whittling away at genuine alternatives until they fit the mold.

One example is Portland's tradition of middle class populism. Since the late nineteenth century, an economy of skilled workers and small businesses has nourished a dissenting political tradition that distrusts professional expertise and corporate leadership. Nearly every mayoral and city council election shows a divide between the outer east side neighborhoods and the central and close-in neighborhoods most benefited by the Goldschmidt package. Issues like sewer infrastructure costs have exacerbated the underlying distrust between the progressive core on the one hand and "country" neighborhoods on the other. In socioeconomic terms, the divide pits anti-tax populists against quality-of-life liberals. However, the city's system of at-large elections combines with its dominant good government ideology to keep such dissent in the minority; it pops up instead in statewide anti-tax movements and in groups such as the Portland Organizing Project that consciously challenge the civic consensus on behalf of the poor.

At the metropolitan scale, a physically compact and institutionally integrated metropolis has left little elbow room for new social and economic interests. In the typical postwar metropolis, new

CONCLUSION

suburban industries have been able to dominate suburban governments in the same way that downtown growth coalitions dominated
central city administrations and politics. One result has been metropolitan fragmentation, but another has been an opportunity for new
voices and forces to enter the political arena. In a sense, loosely knit
metropolitan areas have contributed to political pluralism, perhaps
functioning as political safety valves.

In Portland, older suburbs are partners in the compact city alliance, but they speak more for the classic local growth machine than
for the region's most important new economic interest, the substantial electronics industry in Washington County. Indeed, the industry
has been particularly frustrated by its inability to promote lateral
highways to help get suburban workers to their jobs (see the Westside Bypass story) or to secure local and state funding for a major
engineering school in the western suburbs (being dissatisfied with
the small private Oregon Graduate Institute in Washington County,
with the downtown location of Portland State University, and the
downstate location of Oregon State University).

A third concern is about the balance of reactive politics and moral
politics. The Portland and Oregon style at its best is rational *and*
morally grounded, government by committee and consensus in the
service of the commonweal. An ethic of process that stresses citizen participation and responsibility coexists with an ethic of product that stresses the value of a compact metropolis that sits lightly
on the land. Portland's and Oregon's development history is filled
with moral challenges: the sin of Celilo and the challenge of salmon,
the emotionally charged imperative to save agriculture, the desire
to value the natural environment as a commons. It is filled with rhe-
torical challenges in the language of Old Testament prophets. "Are
you good enough?" asked Lewis Mumford. We need to save the state
from "grasping wastrels," intoned Tom McCall as a moral teacher.

But balancing the community and environmental ethics is also a
politics of socioeconomic resentment and regional chauvinism as a

reaction to globalization and the bureaucracy of the national state. Here we have the failure to dream big dreams, fear of change, and even the historic hope that the Pacific Northwest might be the "best white man's country." Neo-Nazi skinheads have found Portland inhospitable after flourishing there in the 1980s, but the Oregon hills are havens for militant survivalists in whom fears of nuclear disaster and racial war sometimes intermingle.

These sources and voices of dissent notwithstanding, more Portlanders are pragmatists than ideologues. They know they have something special in their metropolis and hope to keep it that way. In 1999, 83 percent of the residents of the City of Portland rated their neighborhood livability "good" or "very good," up from 79 percent in 1994 despite increased concerns about growing traffic congestion and other byproducts of growth.[10] An areawide survey in 1999 found that nearly three times as many residents think Metro is doing a "pretty good" or "excellent" job as rate its performance as poor. Indeed, as pollster Adam Davis points out, the general public is less critical of Metro than are civic leaders.[11]

The larger the scale, however, the more tenuous the institutions and the vaguer the consensus. It is easy to organize around neighborhood stability or around city schools and a city school district, harder to mobilize around the needs of a Willamette Valley or Cascadia. At least for the while, Portland has solved the "planning puzzle" at the city level and is implementing a widely shared vision. At the metropolitan scale we find a more fragile consensus on planning implementation and a public that is divided down the middle in evaluating the growth of the 1990s. At the scale of ecoregions is a powerful but diffuse sense of place without agreement on right action. We know that the Columbia River and its tributaries sustain both economy and culture, but we debate their best use. The very word "forest" elicits deep allegiance, but to multiple ends. Many Portlanders give as much commitment to the Northwest as to their city, but they do not agree on what that "Northwest" is or might become.

How widely can we institutionalize a sense of place? The question again is one of scale. Can we simultaneously value neighborhood, city, metropolitan area, river basin, weekendland, and continental region? One of the issues is incompatible criteria, as we saw in the discussion of Cascadia. Do we define our place as a labor market or an ecological system? And the question is also one of cultural inclusiveness. Can we simultaneously value the natural environment as a source of livelihood and a value in itself, as a site of production and an arena for enjoyment?

The progressive core and many suburbanites have united around the idea of a compact city. The core neighborhoods and the hillsiders can also agree on lifestyle freedom, even if they disagree about resource use. But unheeded interests may also be the sources of new political revolutions. If the Portland consensus erodes and collapses, the probable cause will be challenges from "outsider" groups that see no benefits from public investments and take no pleasure in higher density.

One counter-coalition between east side anti-tax populists and west side high tech entrepreneurs is not likely to be lasting. The two groups in the mid-1990s could agree on opposition to light rail expansion, but their reasons were different. Anti-taxers don't want to spend the money. The electronics lobby want to spend it on something different.

A more likely counter-coalition would combine anti-tax populists with neighborhood activists mobilized to defend moderate income neighborhoods against higher densities and social changes. Such a counter-coalition would raise the banner of status quo against the changes in the urban fabric (and associated costs) required by the vision of a compact city.

We can conclude with education and civic life. From 1940 to 1970,

Oregon was a state that used muscles more than minds, lagging the United States in the percentage of its population with four-year college degrees. The state moved ahead in the 1970s, showed no change in the economically depressed 1980s, and surged again in the 1990s. In 1996, 24 percent of the American population held four-year college degrees, but 34 percent in the Portland area (Multnomah, Washington, Clackamas, and Yamhill Counties).

Along with increasing educational levels is a deep commitment to public schools. In Portland 92 percent of school children attend public schools; the proportion is even higher in the suburbs. Throughout the 1990s, a series of statewide property tax limitation measures shifted school funding from local property taxes to the state legislature, which has offered one-size-fits-all appropriations from the general fund. Metropolitan area parents and school districts in 1999 found themselves begging the legislature and governor—successfully—for the right to tax themselves in excess of statutory limits.

Education is certainly linked to individual achievement and family advancement, but it is also valued as a foundation of community. Education makes for civic interest and knowledgeable participation. What did the staff of the *Willamette Week* newspaper most like about Portland (at least in 1995)? Environmentalism and access to the outdoors, to be sure, but also "the fountain in front of Civic Auditorium. It is an incredible work of art—and you can play in the water." Parks and green shades, to be sure, but also "the best public schools in the country. The best chance to make a difference through citizen involvement." [12] The people of the Portland region engage in intelligent dialogues on community issues ranging from homelessness to suburban growth. They also vote. Both voter registration and voter turnout, calculated as a percentage of those eligible, have run roughly 10 percent higher in Oregon than in the United States as a whole in recent elections (81 percent in November 2000).

"Good citizens are the riches of a city," reads the inscription on the Skidmore Fountain in downtown Portland. Designed by Olin

"Guardians: Under the Lovejoy Ramp" (Georgiana Nehl, painting, 1998, Visual Chronicle of Portland). In the late 1940s and 1950s, a Greek immigrant transformed the support columns for the Lovejoy Street ramp to the Broadway Bridge with religious icons. Shown here in Georgiana Nehl's "Guardians: Under the Lovejoy Ramp," the surviving pictures and their steel columns were saved before the ramp came down in 2000—demolished to make room for high demand downtown housing. The affection toward the columns and the work to save them illustrate the value that Portlanders place on small gestures and individual efforts to enhance the community.

Warner, also known for the bronze entry doors to the Library of Congress, the fountain was erected in 1888 to serve the needs of "horses, men and dogs." The location in the heart of Portland's nineteenth-century business district befuddled *Scribner's* magazine, which thought it would look better in New York's Central Park. Portlanders, however, have always admired the fountain as a symbol of early civic sophistication and the words—by Portland's poetic attorney C. E. S. Wood—as a motto and a challenge.

# NOTES

## Introduction

1. "Portland: Where It Works," *Economist* (Sept. 1, 1990): 24–25.

2. Joan Laatz, "Urban Experts Like Portland's Style," *The Oregonian*, May 6, 1988.

3. For example, recognition by the U.S. Conference on Mayors in 1992; by *Financial World* magazine several times in the 1990s; by Tom McEnery, *The New City-State: Change and Renewal in America's Cities* (Niwot, Colo.: Roberts Rinehart, 1994).

4. Alexander Garvin, *The American City: What Works and What Doesn't* (New York: McGraw-Hill, 1996); Richard Moe and Carter Wilkie, *Changing Places: Rebuilding Community in the Age of Sprawl* (New York: Holt, 1997); Robert Kaplan, *An Empire Wilderness: Travels in America's Future* (New York: Random House, 1998); David Rusk, *Inside Game, Outside Game: Winning Strategies for Saving Urban America* (Washington, D.C.: Brookings Institution Press, 1999), 174; "America's Ten Most Enlightened Towns," *Utne Reader* (June/July 1997); James Howard Kunstler, *The Geography of Nowhere: The Rise and Decline of America's Man-Made Landscape* (New York: Simon and Schuster, 1993), 200.

5. David Broder, "Pioneering Livability," *The Oregonian*, July 15, 1998.

6. Dave Hogan, "Fracturing Our Fabled City," *The Oregonian*, Oct. 3, 1999. For additional positive reviews, see Neal R. Peirce, "Portland Revered as Model," *The Oregonian*, April 3, 1995; Bob Ortega, "Urban Mecca," *Wall Street Journal*, Dec. 26, 1995; Timothy Egan, "Drawing a Hard Line Against Urban Sprawl," *New York Times*, Dec. 30, 1996; David Goldberg, "2 Cities, 2 Routes to the Future," *Atlanta Constitution*, Aug. 28, 1994; E. J. Dionne, "Portland Area Looking Good," *The Oregonian*, March 23, 1997. For negative evaluations, see George Will, "Al

Gore Has a New Worry," *Newsweek* (Feb. 15, 1999); Tim W. Ferguson, "Down with the Burbs! Back to the City!" *Forbes* (May 5, 1997): 142–52.

7. Walter Hines Pages, "The Larger West Coast Cities," *World's Work* (Aug. 10, 1905): 6501; Ray Stannard Baker, "The Great Northwest," *Century Magazine* 65 (March 1903): 659.

8. E. Kimbark MacColl, *The Shaping of a City: Business and Politics in Portland, Oregon, 1885–1915* (Portland: Georgian Press, 1976); E. Kimbark MacColl, *The Growth of a City: Power and Politics in Portland, Oregon, 1915–1950* (Portland: Georgian Press, 1979); E. Kimbark MacColl and Harry Stein, *Merchants, Money and Power: The Portland Establishment, 1843–1913* (Portland: Georgian Press, 1988); Edwin Burrows and Mike Wallace, *Gotham: A History of New York to 1898* (New York: Oxford University Press, 1998).

9. Stewart Holbrook, *The Far Corner: A Personal View of the Pacific Northwest* (New York: Macmillan, 1952), 115.

10. Richard Neuberger, "The Cities of America: Portland, Oregon," *Saturday Evening Post* 219 (March 1, 1947): 22.

11. Rob Eure, "Philanthropy Project Seeks to Tap New Generation of Tech Millionaires," *Wall Street Journal*, Dec. 23, 1996.

12. E. Kimbark MacColl, "Fifty Years of Commission Government," paper delivered at annual meeting of the Pacific Coast Branch-American Historical Association, Eugene, Oregon, August 1981.

13. Freeman Tilden, "Portland, Oregon: Yankee Prudence on the West Coast," *World's Work* 60 (Oct. 1931): 34–40.

14. ‹www.Monk.com/ontheroad/portland/pdxessay/portland.essay.html›.

### Chapter 1. Capital of the Columbia

1. Robin Cody, *Ricochet River* (Portland: Blue Heron Press, 1992), 205.

2. Quoted in David Rusk, *Inside Game, Outside Game: Winning Strategies for Saving Urban America* (Washington, D.C.: Brookings Institution Press, 1999), 177.

3. Robert Ficken, review of Gail Wells, *The Tillamook*, *Oregon Historical Quarterly* 101 (Spring 2000): 97.

4. "The Tillamook Burn," in William Stafford, *Stories That Could Be True: New and Collected Poems* (New York: Harper and Row, 1977), 73.

5. Mathew Deady, "Portland-on-Wallamet," *Overland Monthly* 1 (1868): 43.

6. David James Duncan, *The River Why* (San Francisco: Sierra Club Books, 1983), 252.

7. Stafford, *Stories That Could Be True*, 13.

8. Don Berry, *Trask* (New York: Viking, 1960); H. L. Davis, *Honey in the Horn* (New York: Morrow, 1935), 5; Ken Kesey, *Sometimes a Great Notion* (New York: Viking, 1964), 1, 4–5.

9. Elliott Coues, ed., *History of the Expedition Under the Command of Lewis and Clark* (New York: Dover, 1964), vol. 3, 1248–49; Stephen Dow Beckham, *The Indians of Western Oregon* (Coos Bay: Arago Books, 1977), 58.

10. John K. Townsend, *Narrative of a Journey Across the Rocky Mountains to the Columbia River* [1834], in R. G. Thwaites, ed., *Early Western Travels* (Cleveland, 1904), vol. 21, 301. Also see Gabriel Franchere, *Narrative of a Voyage to the North-west Coast of America in the Years 1811, 1812, 1813, and 1814* [1854], vol. 6, 313: "Leaving the Columbia to ascend the Willamet, I found the banks on either side of that stream well wooded, but low and swampy."

11. Data from manuscript census returns, reported in William A. Bowen, *The Willamette Valley: Migration and Settlement on the Oregon Frontier* (Seattle: University of Washington Press, 1978).

12. Jesse A. Applegate, *Recollections of My Boyhood*, quoted in Howard McKinley Corning, *Willamette Landings: Ghost Towns of the River* (Portland: Binford and Morts, 1947), 16–17.

13. Henry J. Warre and M. Vavasour, "To the Right Honorable the Secretary of State for the Colonies" [Oct. 26., 1845], ed. Joseph Schafer, *Oregon Historical Quarterly* 10 (March 1909): 76.

14. Barry Johnson, "Greg Anthony: On Balancing Sports and Culture," *The Oregonian*, Nov. 12, 1999; Ryan White, "Finding Their Way Around Portland," *The Oregonian*, Nov. 17, 1999.

15. "Ten Things a New Yorker Would Notice About Portland," *Rotund World* 2 (1966): 18–19.

16. John Hamer and Bruce Chapman, *International Seattle: Creating a Globally Competitive Community* (Seattle: Discovery Institute Press, 1992).

17. Davis, *Honey in the Horn*, 329.

18. Amy Kesselman, *Fleeting Opportunities: Women Shipyard Workers in Portland and Vancouver During World War II and Reconversion* (Albany, N.Y.: SUNY Press, 1990), 24.

19. *Oregon Historical Quarterly* 91 (Fall 1990): 285–91.

20. Neil Morgan, *Westward Tilt: The American West Today* (New York: Random House, 1963); Neal Peirce, *The Pacific States of America* (New York: W.W. Norton, 1972); Earl Pomeroy, *The Pacific Slope* (New York: Knopf, 1965); Charles O. Gates and Dorothy Johansen, *Empire of the Columbia* (New York: Harper and Row, 1967), 564.

21. Minutes of Board of Trustees, World Fair Corporation, Jan. 28 and July 22, 1958, Dingwall Papers, University of Washington Manuscripts Division, Seattle.

22. (Port of Seattle) *Reporter*, Feb. 1, 1967, in Port Committee File, Seattle Mayor's Papers, University of Washington Manuscripts Division, Seattle.

23. Calculated from total tonnage and value of shipments as reported in the monthly publication of the U.S. Department of Commerce, *U.S. Waterborne Exports and General Imports*.

24. Mitchell Moss, "Spatial Analysis of the Internet in U.S. Cities and States," Taub Urban Research Center, New York University, 1998, ‹www.urban.nyu/research/newcastle›.

25. Oregon Employment Department, Non-Agricultural Wage and Salary Estimates [covered employment], 1996.

26. U.S. Commerce Department data, reported in Richard Read, "Portland Area Ranks 10th in Exports," *The Oregonian*, Oct. 2,1997.

27. Data from the Internet Organization, ‹www.internet.org›.

28. David Brewster, "Which City Is Better, Seattle or Portland," *The Oregonian*, June 6, 1995; Lizzy Caston, "You Say Monorail, I Say Oregon Trail," *Willamette Week*, Oct. 28, 1998.

29. Ernie Pyle, *Ernie's America: The Best of Ernie Pyle's 1930s Travel Dispatches*, ed. David Nichols (New York: Random House, 1989), 150.

30. Frances Fuller Victor, *Atlantis Arisen, or Talks of a Tourist About Oregon and Washington* (Philadelphia: Lippincott, 1891), 101.

31. *Outside*, June 1992, reported in John Snell, "Magazine; Portland Fourth Best Place

to Live," *The Oregonian*, June 28, 1992; Robin Cody, *Voyage of the Summer Sun: Canoeing the Columbia River* (New York: Knopf, 1995), 276.

32. Brian Booth, ed., *Wildmen, Wobblies and Whistle-Punks: Stewart Holbrook's Lowbrow Northwest* (Corvallis: Oregon State University Press, 1992); James Stevens, *Big Jim Turner* (Garden City, N.Y.: Doubleday, 1948); Molly Gloss, *The Jump-Off Creek* (Boston: Houghton Mifflin, 1989); Craig Lesley, *River Song* (Boston: Houghton Mifflin, 1990) and *The Sky Fisherman* (Boston: Houghton Mifflin, 1995).

33. "Time for a Change? Creating a Pathway to a Knowledge-Creating Region," draft concept paper, Institute for Portland Metropolitan Studies, Portland State University, March 14, 1997.

34. Kathleen Ferguson, "Toward a Geography of Environmentalism in the United States" (M.A. thesis, California State University-Hayward, 1985).

35. Based on holders of hunting and fishing licenses.

36. Oregon Vital Statistics: Annual Report 1993, Table 6-33.

37. David James Duncan, "River Soldiers," *Orion* (Spring 1999): 46.

38. Ursula K. LeGuin, *The Lathe of Heaven* (New York: Scribner, 1971).

39. Ursula K. LeGuin and Roger Dorland, *Blue Moon over Thurman Street* (Portland: New Sage Press, 1993), 37.

40. Employment data from Metro, aggregated by my colleague Tom Sanchez.

41. Keith Moerer, "West Side/East Side," *Willamette Week*, June 11, 1984.

42. Jeff Kuechle, "Civic Schizophrenia: Choosing Up Sides," *The Oregonian*, March 5, 1985.

43. In December 2000 the Clinton administration decided against immediate breaching in favor a complex of other efforts to restore habitat and to protect juvenile salmon on their downstream journeys.

44. Brian Scott and Kim Stafford, *A 25-Year Vision for Central Portland* (Portland: Association for Portland Progress, 1999), 19.

### Chapter 2. Everyday Portlands

1. Median income patterns in the Portland PMSA can be compared with those in twenty-four other MSAs or PMSAs with 1990 populations between 1 million and

2.5 million. Portland's ratio of metrowide family income to central city family income was 1:14, below the middle value for the whole set of metropolitan areas (1:20). Using households rather than families, the metro:city ratio of 1:21 falls below the midpoint for the set (1:28).

2. Recent comparative data on the segregation of the poor identify Portland as one of the most class-integrated metropolitan areas in the country. Working with census tract data, Alan Abramson, Mitchell Tobin, and Matthew VanderGort, in "The Changing Geography of Metropolitan Opportunity: The Segregation of the Poor in U.S. Metropolitan Areas, 1970 to 1990," *Housing Policy Debate* 6 (1995): 45–72, calculated a dissimilarity index and an isolation index for persons below poverty level for each of the 100 largest metropolitan areas in 1990. In 1970, 1980, and 1990 metropolitan Portland had indices substantially below the mean for all large metropolitan areas; its dissimilarity index in 1990 was sixth lowest.

3. Reyner Banham, *Los Angeles: The Architecture of Four Ecologies* (New York: Harper and Row, 1972).

4. Interview with Barbara Roberts, Jan. 13, 2000.

5. Jeff Mapes, "Take a Look in the Mirror, Oregonians," *The Oregonian*, Dec. 19, 1994.

6. Steve Suo and Nena Baker, "Portland Results Reflect Lifestyle, Attitude," *The Oregonian*, Dec. 16, 1996.

7. Nancy Chapman and Joan Starker, "Portland: The Most Livable City?" in *Portland's Changing Landscape*, ed. Larry Price (Portland: Association of American Geographers, 1987), 204.

8. David Sugarman and Murray Straus, "Indicators of Gender Equality for American States and Regions," *Social Indicators Research* 20 (1988): 229–70; Institute for Women's Policy Research, *The Status of Women in Oregon* (Washington, D.C.: the Institute, 1998).

9. Employment data from U.S. Bureau of Labor Statistics; "Women in Business," *The Oregonian*, Oct. 5, 1997.

10. Harvey Scott, *History of Portland* (Syracuse, N.Y.: D. Mason, 1890), 430–31.

11. Frances Fuller Victor, *Atlantis Arisen, or Talks of a Tourist About Oregon and Washington* (Philadelphia: Lippincott, 1891), 89.

12. The Congressional district that stretches from downtown Portland across the West Hills and Washington County to the Pacific shore has elected Democrats since the 1970s, despite the fact that it looks like Republican home ground in its demographics. The rightward movement of the Republican Party in nation and state has helped the Democrats hold the moderate center.

13. Alameda Land Company, *View, Air, Sunshine: A Fitting Homesite—A Golden Investment* (Portland: Alameda Land Company, 1910).

14. Jeffrey M. Berry, Kent E. Portney, and Ken Thomson, *The Rebirth of Urban Democracy* (Washington, D.C.: Brookings Institution Press, 1993). In the later 1980s and 1990s, imperatives of bureaucratic survival in tight budget years caused ONA to push neighborhood associations toward the delivery of services such as crime prevention programs. To a degree, this partial cooptation has undermined the neighborhood association role as advocate for otherwise unheard voices. In the most negative interpretation, ONA management destroyed it in order to save it. In the late 1990s, ONA was renamed the Office of Neighborhood Involvement and its services extended to citizens groups that lack a specific neighborhood base.

15. Julie Sullivan, "Got a Cause? Go to Portland," *The Oregonian*, Nov. 14, 1999.

16. Kristi Turnquist, "Boho: A Lifestyle Thriving in Portland," *The Oregonian*, Feb. 19, 2000.

17. Jeff Hudis, "Boulevard of Bustle," *The Oregonian*, Nov. 5, 1999.

18. Blake Nelson, *Exit* (New York: Scribner's Paperback Fiction, 1997).

19. Comments of Jon Raymond, James Harrison, and Kristin Kennedy at City Club roundtable on "Portland's Emerging Arts Scene," April 6, 2000.

20. Chris Ertel, "Revenge of the Baristas," *Metroscape* 2 (Spring 1996): 6–12.

21. ‹Www.monk.com/ontheroad/portland/pdxguide/guide.htm›; Kristin Foder-Vencil, "Disco Dilemma," *The Oregonian*, Dec. 19, 1994.

22. See ‹www.cityrepair.org/about.htm›.

23. *The Oregonian*, Aug. 12, Oct. 16, 1938.

24. "We're All in This Together: The People of Columbia Villa," brochure from Oregon Council for the Humanities, 1994.

25. Kent Anderson, *Night Dogs* (New York: Bantam Books, 1997), 1.

26. Jeannette Steele, "The Villa: Faces of Hope, Faces of Home," *The Oregonian*, Aug. 29, 1994.

27. Earl Riley to H. H. Jones, July 1, 1943, Earl Riley Papers, Oregon Historical Society, Portland.

28. Elinor Langer, "The American Neo-Nazi Movement Today," *The Nation* 251 (July 16, 1990): 104.

29. Statistics in David Rusk, *Inside Game, Outside Game: Winning Strategies for Saving Urban America* (Washington, D.C.: Brookings Institution Press, 1999), 348–49, 361–63.

30. Lisa Lednicer, "Gresham Fails to Win over Critic Who Deflated Boosters," *The Oregonian*, June 5, 1998.

31. "Tour Story Omitted Positives," *The Oregonian*, July 2, 1998.

32. Joseph Cortright and Heike Mayer, *Portland's Knowledge-Based Economy* (Portland: Institute for Portland Metropolitan Studies, Portland State University, 2000).

33. Oregon Employment Division, Non-Agricultural Wage and Salary Estimates; Joe Cortright and Heike Mayer, *The Ecology of the Silicon Forest* (Portland: Institute for Portland Metropolitan Studies, Portland State University, 2000).

34. Joel Garreau, *Edge City: Life on the New Frontier* (New York: Doubleday, 1991); Robert Cervero, *America's Suburban Centers: The Land Use-Transportation Link* (Boston: Unwin Hyman, 1989).

35. Myron Orfield, *Metropolitics* (Washington, D.C.: Brookings Institution Press, 1997).

36. Susan Orlean, "Figures in a Mall," *New Yorker*, Feb. 1, 1994, 49.

37. Robin Cody, *Ricochet River* (Portland: Blue Heron Press, 1992), 198–99, 202.

38. E. Kimbark MacColl, *Portland: The Growth of a City: Power and Politics in Portland, Oregon, 1915–1950* (Portland: Georgian Press, 1979), 268.

39. Gary Snyder, *The Practice of the Wild: Essays* (San Francisco: North Point Press, 1990), 125.

40. Fred Leeson, "State Farm Revenue Level at $3.38 Billion," *The Oregonian*, Sept. 20, 1997.

41. Foster Church, "Columbia County: Portland's Next Suburb?" *The Oregonian*, Feb. 22, 1998.

42. "Dundee: Residents Get Behind More Tourist-Oriented Goals," *The Oregonian*, Aug. 22, 1999.

43. David James Duncan, *The Brothers K* (New York: Doubleday, 1992), 95.

44. John Painter, Jr., "Grooming Camas for Growth," *The Oregonian*, March 19, 1997.

45. <www.monk.com/ontheroad/portland/pdxguide.html>.

46. Chris Lydgate, "Assault on Tract 86," *Willamette Week*, May 24, 2000.

47. Henry Stein, "Parkrose Stays in the Game," *The Oregonian*, Sept. 10, 1999.

48. Dave Charbonneau, "Tackling a Bad Reputation, the Tigers Trade in Their Black Jerseys," *The Oregonian*, Sept. 8, 1999.


### Chapter 3. The Best Planned City?

1. Elliott Coues, ed., *History of the Expedition Under the Command of Lewis and Clark* (New York: Dover, 1965), vol. 2, 664.

2. *Douglas of the Forests: The North American Journals of David Douglas*, ed. John Davies (Seattle: University of Washington Press, 1980), 41.

3. Alexander Ross, *Adventures of the First Settlers on the Oregon or Columbia River* (London: Smith and Elder, 1849), 118.

4. Richard Neuberger, *Our Promised Land* (New York: Macmillan, 1938); Robert Ormond Case, *River of the West: A Study of Opportunity in the Columbia Empire* (Portland: Northwestern Electric Company and Pacific Power and Light Company, 1940); Murray Morgan, *The Columbia: Powerhouse of the West* (Seattle: Superior Publishing, 1949).

5. Quoted in Elizabeth Woody and Gloria Bird, "Dancing on the Rim of the World," in *Varieties of Hope: An Anthology of Oregon Prose*, ed. Gordon Dodds (Corvallis: Oregon State University Press, 1993), 139.

6. Craig Lesley, *River Song* (New York: Picador, 1999), 68.

7. David James Duncan, "River Soldiers," *Orion* (Spring 1999): 38–39.

8. "Interim Report on Journal Building Site Use and Waterfront Development," Portland City Club *Bulletin* 50 (August 8, 1969).

9. Neal R. Peirce, *The Pacific States of America* (New York: W.W. Norton, 1972), 215; Nancy Chapman and Joan Starker, "Portland: The Most Livable City?" in *Portland's Changing Landscape*, ed. Larry Price (Portland: Association of American Geographers, 1987), 204.

10. Richard Neuberger, "The Cities of America: Portland, Oregon," *Saturday Evening Post* 219 (March 1, 1947): 22–23.

11. "Remarks of Sally Landauer," June 14, 1994, ‹www.pdxplan.org/LandauerWeb.html›.

12. Interview with Allison Belcher, June 20, 2000.

13. Allison Belcher interview; Marjorie Gustafson, interview by Ernie Bonner, August 1995, ‹www.pdxplan.org/GustafsonWeb1.html›.

14. Bob Baldwin, interview by Ernie Bonner, Dec. 30, 1994, ‹www.pdxplan.org/BaldwinWeb.html›.

15. W. A. Henry III, "Portland Offers a Calling Card," *Time* 132 (Dec. 12, 1988): 88; Philip Langdon, "How Portland Does It," *Atlantic Monthly* (Nov. 1992): 134–41; Donald Canty, "Portland," *Architecture: The AIA Journal* 75 (July 1986): 32–47; Berton Roueche, "A New Kind of City," *New Yorker*, Oct. 21, 1985, 42–53; Sam Hall Kaplan, "Portland Sets Example in Urban Design," *Los Angeles Times*, Sept. 24, 1989; Neal R. Peirce and Robert Guskind, *Breakthroughs: Re-Creating the American City* (New Brunswick, N.J.: Center for Urban Policy Research, Rutgers University, 1993).

16. Robert D. Kaplan, "Travels into America's Future," *Atlantic Monthly* (Aug. 1998): 58; Robert Shibley, quoted in Peirce and Guskind, *Breakthroughs*, 80; Robert Bruegmann, "New Centers on the Periphery," *Center: A Journal for Architecture in America* 7 (1992): 25–43.

17. Gideon Bosker and Lena Lencek, *Frozen Music: A History of Portland Architecture* (Portland: Oregon Historical Society, 1985), xiv.

18. Data from Metro and Portland Development Commission, summarized in Carl Abbott, Gerhard Pagenstecher, and Britt Parrott, *Trends in Portland's Central City, 1970–98* (Portland: Association for Portland Progress, 1998).

19. Edgar Hoover and Raymond Vernon, *Anatomy of a Metropolis: The Changing Distribution of People and Jobs Within the New York Metropolitan Region* (Cambridge, Mass.: Harvard University Press, 1959).

20. Interview with Jane Cease, June 13, 2000.

21. Mary Pedersen-Blackett, interview by Ernie Bonner, Dec. 1999, ‹www.pdxplan.org/BlackettWeb1.html›.

22. Fred Leeson, "Don't Brush Off Interstate MAX Opposition," *The Oregonian*, Feb. 28, 2000.

23. Dan Gorman, letter to *The Oregonian*, Feb 22, 2000.

24. In fact, vacant lot infill, accessory apartments attached to single family houses, and similar options will account for only a small fraction of Portland's planned addition of 71,000 dwelling units. A group of civic leaders recently suggested that the city back off from pushing such neighborhood infill because the political cost of decreasing support for city planning is not worth the incremental gain in density. City Club of Portland, *Increasing Density in Portland* (Portland: City Club, 1999).

25. Timothy Egan, "In Portland, Houses Are Friendly. Or Else," *New York Times*, April 20, 2000.

26. Quoted in Brent Walth, *Fire at Eden's Gate: Tom McCall and the Oregon Story* (Portland: Oregon Historical Society, 1994), 356.

27. Carl Abbott and Margery Post Abbott, *Historical Development of the Metropolitan Service District* (Portland: Metro Home Rule Charter Committee, 1991), 22.

28. Carl Abbott and Deborah Howe, "The Politics of Land-Use Law in Oregon: Senate Bill 100, Twenty Years After," *Oregon Historical Quarterly* 94 (Spring 1993): 10.

29. The UGB is not a "great wall of Portland" as sometimes described by its critics. A better analogy is a skin that contains the vital functions of an organism but expands as the organism expands. Similarly, the UGB is expected to expand gradually as the metropolis grows. As Linda Johnson has noted, those with a literary bent might liken Portland to Italo Calvino's "invisible city" of Olinda: "Olinda is certainly not the only city that grows in concentric circles, like tree trunks which each year add one more ring. But in other cities there remains, in the center, the old narrow girdle of walls from which the withered spires rise, the towers, the tiled roofs, the domes, while the new quarters sprawl around them like a loosened belt. Not Olinda: the old walls expand bearing the old quarters with them, enlarged, but maintaining their proportions on a broad horizon at the edges of the city; they surround the slightly newer quarters, which also grew up on the margins and became thinner to make room for still more recent ones pressing from inside; and so, on and on." Advocates of growth management argue that "Olinda" is far superior to the suburban sprawl of a city like Calvino's Penthesilea, where "you advance for hours and it is not clear to you whether you are already in the city's midst or still outside it. Like a lake with low shores lost in swamps, so Penthesilea spreads for miles around, a soupy city diluted on the

plain; pale buildings back to back in mangy fields . . . a street of scrawny shops which fades amid patches of leprous countryside." Italo Calvino, *Invisible Cities,* trans. William Weaver (San Diego: Harcourt Brace Jovanovich, 1974), 129, 156–57.

30. The movement toward fair share housing suffered a setback in 1999, when the state prohibited mandatory inclusionary zoning. Metro had been considering a requirement that new development include a specified percentage of dwellings affordable to low and moderate income households (as is the case, for example, in Montgomery County, Maryland). Homebuilders convinced the legislature and governor that such a requirement would be one intervention too many in the real estate market, leaving Metro's *Regional Affordable Housing Strategy* (June 2000) to call rather plaintively for voluntary inclusionary measures.

31. Quoted in Alan Ehrenhalt, "The Great Wall of Portland," *Governing* 10 (May 1997): 23.

32. "Yes for Roads and Rail," *The Oregonian,* Oct. 17, 1996.

33. Randy Gragg, "Linda K. Johnson: On Interpreting Urban Growth," *The Oregonian,* Oct. 15, 1999.

34. Judith Berck, "Driving on Portland's Urban Growth Boundary," *Oregon Humanities* (Spring 2000): 36.

35. The provisions of the Urban Growth Management Functional Plan include (1) housing and job targets for each of the area's twenty-four cities and incorporated portions of three counties that will require higher overall densities; (2) requirements for minimum development densities for new housing averaging 80 percent of the zoned maximum; (3) exclusion of big box retailing from industrial zones; (4) minimum and maximum parking ratios for new development; (5) a requirement that Metro develop specific affordable housing goals; (6) a provision for UGB expansion if enough communities demonstrate that the targets won't work. Critics argue that the plan actually involves substantial and unworkable increases from the density increases approved in the 2040 Growth Concept.

36. Data from Metro's Growth Management Section. Until these very recent changes in development patterns, the Portland region was growing more *compactly* than many other metropolitan regions but not more *densely.*

37. Joint Center for Housing Studies, *The State of the Nation's Housing, 1996: Portland Metropolitan Area Profile* (Cambridge, Mass.: Harvard University, 1997).

38. James Mayer, "Home Taxes Soar in North, Northeast," *The Oregonian*, Oct. 20, 1996.

39. For a discussion of the arguments about the urban growth boundary and housing affordability, see Carl Abbott, "Planning a Sustainable City: The Promise and Performance of Portland's Urban Growth Boundary," in *Urban Sprawl: Causes, Consequences, and Policy Responses*, ed. Gregory D. Squires (Washington, D.C.: Urban Institute Press, 2001). For opposing explanations of price inflation, also see Sam Staley and Gerard C. S. Mildner, *Urban Growth Boundaries and Housing Affordability* (Los Angeles: Reason Public Policy Institute, 1999) and Justin Phillips and Eban Goodstein, "Growth Management and Housing Prices: The Case of Portland, Oregon," *Contemporary Economic Policy* 18 (July 2000): 334–44.

40. Gordon Oliver, "Apartment Hunters Move In on Deals," *The Oregonian*, Dec. 6, 1999.

41. 1000 Friends of Oregon, *Willamette County News* 2 (Sept. 1995): 1.

42. John Jackley, "Endangered Species," *The Oregonian*, Nov. 24, 1996; "Metro: Tigard Takes Issue with Growth Blueprint," *The Oregonian*, Sept. 3, 1996.

43. Lewis Mumford, *Regional Planning in the Pacific Northwest: A Memorandum* (Portland: Northwest Regional Council, 1939).

44. Katherine Dunn, "Why I Live in Portland," in Dodds, *Varieties of Hope*, 65–66.

45. Oregon Planning Board, *Second Report on Willamette Valley* (Salem: Planning Board, 1937), 62.

46. ‹www.econ.state.or.us/wvlf/execpage.htm›.

47. Frances Fuller Victor, *Atlantis Arisen, or Talks of a Tourist About Oregon and Washington* (Philadelphia: J. P. Lippincott, 1891), 54.

48. "Hatfield Makes Gorge Stop," *Gorge Weekly*, June 9, 1995.

49. Thomas Vaughan and Terence O'Donnell, *Portland: An Informal History and Guide* (Portland: Oregon Historical Society, 1984), 17.

50. Glen Coffield, "Crossing Hawthorne Bridge," *Northwest Poems* (Portland: Rose City Publisher, 1954), in *From Here We Stand: An Anthology of Oregon Poetry*, ed. Ingrid Wendt and Primus St. John (Corvallis: Oregon State University Press, 1993), 127.

51. "Winter Fog Along the Willamette," in Wendt and St. John, *From Here We Stand*, 167–68.

52. U.S. Congress, House, Committee on Industrial Arts and Expositions, "Lewis and Clark Centennial Exposition: Hearings Before the House of Representatives Committee on Industrial Arts and Expositions," 58th Cong., 2nd Sess., Jan 14, 1904, p. 27; Robertus Lowe, "The Lewis and Clark Fair," *World's Work* 10 (Aug. 1905): 6458.

53. Hubert Howe Bancroft, *The New Pacific*, rev. ed. (New York: Bancroft, 1913), 8, 9, 13.

54. Data from Port of Portland.

55. See "Regional Connections," a 1997 report from the Institute for Portland Metropolitan Studies, Portland State University.

56. Ernest Callenbach, *Ecotopia* (Berkeley, Calif.: Banyan Tree Press, 1975).

57. Peter K. Schoonmaker, Bettina von Hagen, and Edward C. Wolf, *The Rain Forests of Home* (Washington, D.C.: Island Press, 1997).


**Conclusion**

1. ‹www.monk.com/ontheroad/portland/pdxessay/portland.essay.html›.

2. Ernie Pyle, *Ernie's America: The Best of Ernie Pyle's 1930s Travel Dispatches*, ed. David Nichols (New York: Random House, 1989), 150.

3. Blake Nelson, *Exile* (New York: Scribner Paperback Fiction, 1997), 232.

4. Filmmaker Todd Haynes, quoted in Shawn Levy, "That Portland Vibe," *The Oregonian*, July 23, 2000.

5. Philip Langdon, "How Portland Does It," *Atlantic Monthly* (Nov. 1992): 134–42.

6. Arthur Louis, "The Worst American City," *Harper's* 50 (Jan. 1975): 67–71; Ben-Chieh Liu, *Quality of Life Indicators in U.S. Metropolitan Areas, 1970: A Comprehensive Assessment* (Washington, D.C.: U. S. Environmental Protection Agency, 1975).

7. "The Best Cities for Business," *Fortune* (Oct. 23, 1989): 82.

8. Robert Kaplan, "Travels into America's Future," *Atlantic Monthly* (Aug. 1998): 58.

9. "Where Charity Begins," *Governing* 12 (August 1999): 13.

10. Portland City Auditor, "City of Portland Service Efforts and Accomplishments, 1998–99," ‹www.ci.portland.or.us'auditor/pdxaudit.htm›.

11. Adam Davis, personal communication.

12. *Willamette Week*, Nov. 14, 1995.

# INDEX

Page numbers in italics refer to illustrations.

# ACKNOWLEDGMENTS

This book owes much to Judith Martin and Sam Bass Warner, Jr., who developed the idea of a series of metropolitan portraits and who have read the manuscript with a careful eye. Other participants in a University of Minnesota workshop on the project—Larry Ford, Dan Arreola, and Dana White—helped clarify my ideas.

In Portland, I am grateful to the staff of the Oregon Historical Society and the city's Archives and Records Center for assistance with research over more than twenty years. Historian E. Kimbark MacColl is unfailingly generous with his unsurpassed knowledge of Portland politics. Urban consultant David Rusk and Portlanders Ethan Seltzer, Adam Davis, and Brian Booth read and commented on the manuscript as a whole. Because the interpretation builds on a number of previous articles and chapters I have published, I have also benefited from the comments of editors and reviewers too numerous to mention.

Portland has a strong tradition of informed reporting on local issues, and I have profited from a quarter century of careful reading of *The Oregonian* and *Willamette Week*.

Because I have tried to embed my analysis of Portland in its rich regional culture, I want to thank the writers, artists, and designers whose work has informed and sometimes structured my analysis. Individual artists and designers who have shared images of their work include David McCloskey, Mark Lakeman, Barry Peril, Linda Johnson, Yalcin Erhan, and Robert Murase. I very much appreciate the efforts of Peggy Kendellen, public art coordinator for the Regional Arts and Culture Council, to furnish images from the Visual Chronicle of Portland. My colleague Irina Sharkova prepared the maps of the Columbia River, the CMSA, and the municipalities of the PMSA.

I also wish to thank Tim Barnes for permission to reproduce "Winter Fog Along the Wilamette"; Judith Burck for permission to reproduce "Driving Portland's Urban Growth Boundary," which first appeared in the *Oregon Humanities Journal*; Kim Stafford for permission to quote lines from the Central City Summit; the Estate of William Stafford for permission to reproduce "My Party the Rain," copyright 1997 William Stafford, from *Stories That Could Be True* (Harper and Row); and *Orion* magazine for permission to reproduce excerpts from David James Duncan, "River Soldiers."

For further reading about Portland and its region, visit ‹www.upa.pdx.edu/USP/faculty/carls_guide.html›

ACKNOWLEDGMENTS